P R O F E S S I O N A L

Hong Kong Patent Law

G U I D E

Averil C Waters

FT
LAW & TAX
Asia Pacific

Published by **FT Law & Tax Asia Pacific**
An imprint of **Pearson Professional Asia Pacific**

Suite 1808
Asian House
1 Hennessy Road
Wan Chai
Hong Kong
Tel: (852) 2863 2600
Fax: (852) 2520 6646
Internet: pphkg@hk.super.net
Web: www.pearson-pro.com.hk

First published 1997

Printed in Hong Kong

ISBN 962 661 065 4

Preface

This book is intended to be a practical guide to the patent law in Hong Kong for those interested in the protection of inventions in Hong Kong whether they are from Hong Kong or from overseas. While the book is likely to be of particular interest to intellectual property practitioners in Hong Kong, it also caters for inventors and practitioners in other countries or jurisdictions who want to have a general understanding of Hong Kong's patent system.

I want to emphasise the evolutionary nature of the changes to the patent system in Hong Kong and place the changes in the international context. This book therefore covers the old law and sets out in some detail the background leading to the introduction of the new patent system and the report of the Patents Steering Committee.

For anyone who merely wants to have a general overview of the patent system then Chapters 3 and 4 give a general outline of the old law, the new law and the transitional provisions. These chapters are intended to answer basic questions on the new system. In addition, Chapters 11 to 14 provide a summary of the main features of the new law in an easy to read format.

For those who are looking for a more detailed coverage of the practical aspects and on the transitional provisions, then Chapters 5 to 6 provide this. The transitional provisions are covered in Chapter 5. These provisions will affect patents and applications for patents for some years to come due to the time between application and publication and subsequent grant. Owners of patents or patent applications which could have been protected under the old law should be aware of these provisions if they wish to protect their inventions in Hong Kong.

The application procedure for a standard patent and a short-term patent are dealt with in Chapters 9 to 10. As this is a practical guide the emphasis is on the steps and procedures for filing applications and the time periods which apply.

Chapters 7 and 8 go through the *Patents Ordinance* and the *Patents (General) Rules* section by section. This is intended as a guide to users by highlighting the relevant aspects of the Ordinance and the Rules which cover any particular subject matter.

The reform exercise has been a long process and I want to take this opportunity to acknowledge those who contributed to the reform exercise. This includes the members of the original Patents Working Group, the Patents Steering Committee itself which met on over 100 occasions, the consultants who commented on the Patents Steering Committee Report and other proposals and all those involved in the preparation of the new law and its introduction.

As I was involved in the proposal for the changes to the patent system for many years I want to express my appreciation and thanks to all those on the Patents Steering Committee and in the Hong Kong Government with whom I shared this experience particularly my former colleagues in the former Registrar General's Department and the Intellectual Property Department and Jonothan Abbott of the Department of Justice.

Averil C Waters
Nov 1977

Contents

Patents Ordinance

Patent (General) Rules

Registration of Patents Ordinance

Patents (Transitional Arrangements) Rules

1 Introduction

The patent system in Hong Kong is designed to protect inventions and new technical ideas, which are of practical use. An invention to be capable of being protected must be new, involve an inventive step and be industrially applicable. The patent system both under the former law and the new law also reflects an important tenet of patent systems worldwide, namely, that an inventor in exchange for his patent must make the details of the invention available to the public.

Old Law

The former patent system in Hong Kong dates back to 1932. The old patent law as contained in the *Registration of Patents Ordinance* (Chapter 42), provided for the registration of patents granted by the United Kingdom Patent Office. This included both United Kingdom patents granted under the United Kingdom *Patents Act* of 1949 and 1977 and European patents granted under the European Patent Convention designating the United Kingdom which took effect under the *Patents Act* 1977. On registration the patent remained in force for so long as it was in force in the United Kingdom. The patent proprietor had the same rights as if it had been granted in the United Kingdom with an extension to Hong Kong. The *Patents Act* 1977 and the European Patent Convention protects all types of inventions which are new, involve an inventive step and which are industrially applicable. It follows that patents registered in Hong Kong are based on these criteria. The former system was a registration system dependent, both before and after registration in Hong Kong, on the United Kingdom patent system. The *Registration of Patents Ordinance* was repealed on the 28 June 1997 when the new law came into operation.

New Law

The *Patents Ordinance* (No 52 of 1997) was enacted on 28 May 1997 and came into operation on the 27 June 1997. The introduction of the *Patents Ordinance* heralds a new era for the patent system in Hong Kong. The Ordinance provides for the grant of an independent patent in Hong Kong based on the grant of patents granted by designated patent offices. The patent when granted will be capable of being tested for validity, enforced, amended and rectified in Hong Kong independent of action taken in any other jurisdiction in respect of the patent on which the grant in Hong Kong was based. The Ordinance also provides for the grant of a short-term patent on original application in Hong Kong. The short-term patent will be a new type of protection for Hong Kong and will protect inventions with a short-term commercial life.

Evolutionary Approach

It is important to emphasize that the new patent law takes an evolutionary approach. In some areas the new law breaks new ground but in others it reflects and codifies the old law. This ensures continuity between the old and new law.

Similarities Between Old Law and New Law

As regards the patentability of an invention there will be no change. The new law will continue to protect inventions which are new, involve an inventive step and which are industrially applicable. The rights and remedies given to the proprietor of a patent will also remain largely unchanged, but they have been codified to reflect and enhance the existing law. There will continue to be no original application for the grant of a patent in Hong Kong except in the case of a short-term patent for which original application can be made in Hong Kong.

Differences Between Old Law and New Law

The procedures for obtaining a patent are new and differ from the former procedures. Thus the time for filing an application for a patent and the procedural requirements on making an application are different. The time for filing is substantially reduced. Under the old law a patent owner had five years after the grant of the patent in the United Kingdom Patent Office in which to file in Hong Kong. This has been reduced to a period of six months after publication of the application for the patent by the designated patent office.

The status of the patent when granted in Hong Kong is likewise new. Under the new law the patent will be independent of the patent granted by the designated patent office on which the patent was based. This means that under the new law the patent will be capable of being amended and revoked in Hong Kong.

In an important departure from the old law, the new law provides that the patent will have to be renewed in Hong Kong to continue to be protected. This will be a significant change for proprietors and patent practitioners.

Guide to Content

This book is intended to be a practical guide to the patent law.

Chapter 2 gives the background to the new law and deals with

- the old law including its history and effect;
- the factors for change which includes the effect of the Sino-British Joint Declaration and the Basic Law and the international treaties;
- the setting up of the Patents Steering Committee and its Report; and
- the proposals for the new law, the legislation and the legislative history.

Chapter 3 provides an overview of the *Registration of Patents Ordinance* and the old law and an outline of the *Patents Ordinance* and *Patents (General) Rules* and the transitional provisions.

Chapter 4 sets out the main aspects of the new law.

Chapter 5 deals with the transitional provisions as provided for in the *Patents Ordinance* and the *Patents (Transitional Arrangements) Rules.*

Chapter 6 outlines some of the practical aspects of change particularly as it relates to the procedural requirements and the transitional provisions and sets out some of the key dates which may be a trigger for subsequent action or which are due dates for taking action.

Chapter 7 gives an overall explanation of the *Patents Ordinance* and *Patents (General) Rules* section by section. It expands on the outline given in Chapter 3 by giving greater detail on the contents of each part by reference to each section.

Chapter 8 deals with the application procedures for the standard patent.

Chapter 9 deals with the short-term patent including the application procedures.

Chapters 10 to 14 set out the main features of the new law and the transitional provisions at a glance.

In most cases when reference is made to the new law this will include a reference to the *Patents Ordinance* and the subsidiary legislation made under the *Patents Ordinance*. Similarly reference to the old law means a reference to the *Registration of Patents Ordinance* and its subsidiary legislation including as relevant the effect of the old law as established by the case law. In referring to the *Patents (General) Rules* and *Patents (Transitional Arrangements) Rules* made under the *Patents Ordinance* reference will be to the *Patents Rules* and to the *Transitional Rules* respectively. References to the masculine include the feminine.

2 Background to the New Law

This Chapter deals with the old law, including its history and effect. It sets out the factors for change, which include consideration of the old law, the effect of the Sino-British Joint Declaration and the Basic Law and international treaties. It covers the setting up of the Patents Steering Committee and the content and recommendations of its report in respect of patents, petty patents, the Technical Information Centre and the consultation process. The proposals for the new law and the historical steps leading to the introduction of the new law are outlined.

The *Registration of Patents Ordinance* provided for the protection of inventions in Hong Kong. The Patents Registry administered the Ordinance, which is part of the Intellectual Property Department of the Hong Kong Government. The *Patents Ordinance* introduces no change to the administration of the patent law and it will continue to be administered by an expanded Patents Registry. The Director of Intellectual Property will continue to be the Registrar of Patents.

The *Registration of Patents Ordinance* was first enacted in 1932 and has been amended on a number of occasions. The Ordinance was amended in 1968 to provide for Crown use by the addition of ss 7A to 7D of the *Registration of Patents Ordinance*. Sections 7A to 7D were repealed and replaced in 1996 by the *Intellectual Property (World Trade Organisation Amendments) Ordinance* to bring the provisions in line with the requirements of the Agreement on Trade Related Aspects of Intellectual Property. The provisions, as amended, allow for government use only after the declaration of a period of urgency made by the Governor-in-Council. These provisions have not in fact been used. The Ordinance was substantially amended in 1979 to reflect the changes introduced in the United Kingdom by the *Patents Act* 1977 and to allow for the registration of European patents designating the United Kingdom which take effect under that Act.

The *Registration of Patents Ordinance* provided for the registration in Hong Kong of patents granted under the United Kingdom *Patents Acts* of 1949 and 1977. This included European patents granted under the European Patent Convention designating the United Kingdom, which took effect pursuant to s 77 of the *Patents Act* 1977 (s 2 of the *Registration of Patents Ordinance*). Application for registration in Hong Kong had to be made within five years of the grant of the patent by the United Kingdom Patent Office (s 3 *Registration of Patents Ordinance*). The application had to be accompanied by a certified copy of the patent specification, a translation (if it was published in a language other than English) and a certificate giving full particulars of the grant by the United Kingdom Comptroller-General of Patents Designs and Trademarks (s 4 *Registration of Patents Ordinance*). If the formality requirements were complied with the Registrar had to register the patent and issue a certificate of registration (s 5 *Registration of Patents Ordinance*). On registration and issue of the certificate the proprietor had the same rights as if the patent had been granted in the United Kingdom with an extension to Hong Kong *(s 6 Registration of Patents Ordinance).* The patent remained in force so long as the application remained in force in the United Kingdom (s 7 *Registration of Patents Ordinance).*

Application Procedures

The *Registration of Patents Ordinance* and Rule 2 of the *Registration of Patents Rules* set out the basic filing requirements. There were no prescribed forms and the Ordinance and Rules were short on detail. In practice an applicant was required to file:

- A certified copy of the specification of the patent (including drawings, if any) and, if it was not published in English, a certified copy of the translation into English;
- A certificate from the United Kingdom Comptroller giving full particulars of the grant of the patent;
- A statutory declaration setting out the interest and title of the applicant; and
- A fee which was prior to repeal set at HK$1,800.

Post Registration Requirements

Amendments

The *Registration of Patents Ordinance* contained provisions that allowed for recording amendments to the specification or drawing of the registered patent if it had been amended or treated as amended according to the law in the United Kingdom (s 9 *Registration of Patents Ordinance*). Thus on such amendment in the United Kingdom a proprietor was able to file a request with the Registrar to substitute the amended specification and drawings for those filed. A copy of the amendments and any translation certified by the United Kingdom Comptroller had to accompany such request.

Registration of assignment, transmission or other instrument

The *Registration of Patents Ordinance* contained provisions allowing any person who became entitled to a patent registered in Hong Kong by assignment, transmission or operation of law to make application for the entry on the register of such assignment, transmission or other instrument. Every application had to be accompanied by a statutory declaration setting out the interest and title of the applicant and an original or certified copy of every document on which the applicant's title depended (s 10 *Registration of Patents Ordinance* and Rule 4 of the *Registration of Patents Rules*).

General

There was no requirement to renew the patent in Hong Kong but the patent had to be renewed in the United Kingdom Patent Office to remain in force and so continue to be protected in Hong Kong. There were no provisions that allowed for the status of the patent in the United Kingdom Patent Office to be recorded in the Register. Thus there was no record in the Hong Kong register of patents as to whether or not the patent was renewed or revoked in the United Kingdom. Any person wishing to establish the status of a patent in Hong Kong had to search in both the Hong Kong Patents Registry and the United Kingdom Patent Office. As there was no obligation on registered proprietors to register assignments and amendments to the patent specification or drawings it was always advisable to search in the United Kingdom Patent Office for such information as well.

Public Search

The register of patents and the patent specification can be searched at the Patents Registry. The register and search card index were maintained manually by the Hong Kong Patents Registry and, whilst details of the proprietor and the patent could be obtained, the ability to carry out any detailed search for novelty was curtailed by the limitations of the search facility. The Register has recently been computerised, but some old data will still only be available in manual form.

Effect of Old Law

The *Registration of Patents Ordinance* was commendable for its brevity but it created some uncertainties, particularly with the introduction in the United Kingdom of the *Patents Act* 1977, which replaced the prerogative rights of the Crown in relation to patents with a statutory framework and code. The effect of the provisions of the Ordinance was, as a result, in some respects unclear. In one respect it was clear, in that the *Registration of Patents Ordinance* did not apply the *Patents Act* 1977 to Hong Kong. The courts in both the United Kingdom and Hong Kong have considered the effect of s 6 of the *Registration of Patents Ordinance.*

In the most recent decision in *Canon Kabushiki Kaisha v Green Cartridge Company (Hong Kong) Ltd. and Anor*[1] Mr Justice Rogers at the first instance considered this question (pp 882 to 888). He considered the history of the *Registration of Patents Ordinance* and noted that the *Patents Act* 1977 replaced the grant of a monopoly by the Crown with a statutory code defining the rights and remedies of a patentee. As a result, he concluded that, because some of the provisions of the *Patents Act* 1977 were specifically limited to the United Kingdom, difficulties arose in interpreting which of those provisions had effect in Hong Kong by virtue of the *Registration of Patents Ordinance*. Mr Justice Rogers held that it was certainly understood that a proprietor of a United Kingdom patent could, on adopting the appropriate procedure in Hong Kong, have the same rights and privileges in Hong Kong as he had in the United Kingdom in respect of his patent. In assessing which parts of the *Patents Act* 1977 took effect in Hong Kong, he held that it was only those parts of the *Patents Act* 1977 that governed the rights and privileges of the patentee. He concluded that this accordingly gave a patentee the right to seek relief in the Hong Kong court to restrain infringement. He concluded, however, that this was as far as it went and that there was no power vested in the Hong Kong court to amend or revoke a patent.

Summary

In summary, the effect of the old law was that:

- Patents granted by the United Kingdom Patent Office pursuant to the *Patents Acts* 1949 and 1977, including European Patents designating the United Kingdom, could be registered in Hong Kong;
- Application for registration could be made at any time within five years after grant of the patent by the United Kingdom Patent Office but could not be made after that period had expired;
- Upon issue of the certificate of registration in Hong Kong, the proprietor of the patent had the same rights as if the patent had been granted in the United Kingdom with an extension to Hong Kong. It was understood that this had the effect of enabling a proprietor of a patent registered in Hong Kong to bring an action for infringement in Hong Kong on the basis of the right to obtain such relief granted by the United Kingdom *Patents Act* 1977;
- The patent remained in force so long as it was in force in the United Kingdom;
- A patent had to be renewed in the United Kingdom to remain in force in Hong Kong;
- A patent registered in Hong Kong could not be revoked or amended by the Hong Kong courts;
- No record of the status of a patent in the United Kingdom was made in the register maintained by the Hong Kong Patents Registry;
- The Registrar maintained a register giving details of the registered proprietor, the title of the invention and other relevant data;
- Assignments or other transactions could be recorded on such register at the option of the proprietor; and
- Amendments made to the specification could be recorded with the Registrar at the option of the proprietor.

Factors for Change

Old Law

The old law provided Hong Kong with a well-respected, cost effective patent system with fully searched and examined patents that were in line with international standards. The application procedures were relatively straightforward and cost effective. These advantages were, however, outweighed by a number of less positive factors.

One area of concern was the long time period before application for protection had to be made in Hong Kong. This was clearly of benefit to patent proprietors but created problems for other users of the patent system. In practice this meant that there was no information available in Hong Kong as to whether a patent granted in the United Kingdom was to be protected here until the five year period had elapsed.

Another factor was the dependency on the United Kingdom patent after grant and the lack of information in Hong Kong as to the current status of the patent. Added to this were the uncertainties of the effect of the old law as outlined above. Taking all these factors into account it was clear that Hong Kong needed to modernise its patent law.

Sino-British Joint Declaration and the Basic Law

No discussion on the new patent law would be complete without reference to the resumption of sovereignty over Hong Kong by China on 1 July 1997. The Sino-British Joint Declaration[2] and the Basic Law of the Hong Kong Special Administrative Region[3] provided the basis for the Hong Kong Special Administrative Region when China resumed sovereignty on 1 July 1997.

The Sino-British Joint Declaration and the Basic Law in general provide for the Hong Kong Special Administrative Region to enjoy a high degree of autonomy in trade and economic affairs and for the continued application of laws previously in force, including common law rules.

As regards international treaties the Sino-British Joint Declaration and the Basic Law contain provisions which allow for the continued application of international agreements to the Hong Kong Special Administrative Region after 1 July 1997. The Hong Kong

Special Administrative Region continues as a member of the World Trade Organisation in its own right and Article 139 of the Basic Law is of particular relevance to the Hong Kong patent system. This Article provides that the Government of the Hong Kong Special Administrative Region shall, on its own, formulate policies on science and technology and protect by law achievements in scientific and technological research, patents, discoveries and inventions.

Thus the Hong Kong Special Administrative Region Government is required to maintain its own separate intellectual property regime and, in particular, its own patent laws. In view of the fact that the old law was dependent on the United Kingdom patent system there was a clear need to modernise and localise Hong Kong's patent law.

Discussions took place in the Sino-British Joint Liaison Group to consider the new patent law proposals and the continued application of relevant intellectual property law treaties. The Hong Kong Government has confirmed that agreement was reached in November 1995[4] over patent law proposals. These have been embodied in the *Patents Ordinance*. It was also agreed that the Paris Convention and the Patent Cooperation Treaty would continue to apply to the Hong Kong Special Administrative Region after 1 July 1997. This means that the *Patents Ordinance* continues in force despite the change in sovereignty.

International Treaties

Paris Convention and the Patent Cooperation Treaty

The Convention for the Protection of Industrial Property 1883 as revised (the Paris Convention) and the Patent Cooperation Treaty (the PCT) are the main intellectual property treaties dealing with patents. Both are administered by the World Intellectual Property Organisation. Both the United Kingdom and China are party to these treaties. Only states may be members and parties to these treaties. However, any member may inform the Director-General of the World Intellectual Property Organisation by written notification at any time that the treaties may be applied to all or any part of those territories for which it is responsible.

The United Kingdom applied both the Paris Convention and the PCT to Hong Kong in 1977 and 1981 respectively. As indicated, the Sino-British Joint Liaison Group reached agreement for the continued application of these treaties to Hong Kong. It is assumed that the methodology of such application will be part of the overall application of the Sino-British Joint Declaration as it relates to Hong Kong's treaty obligations.

World Trade Organisation and the Agreement on Trade Related Aspects of Intellectual Property

The Treaty establishing the World Trade Organisation was signed in 1993 and came into effect on 1 January 1995. The Agreement on Trade Related Aspects of Intellectual Property (TRIPs Agreement) was established by the World Trade Organisation.

The TRIPs Agreement sets the requirements for all types of intellectual property. Part I of the TRIPs Agreement sets out the general provisions and principles and in particular the important doctrines of national treatment and most favoured nation treatment. Part II sets standards concerning the availability, scope and use of intellectual property rights. Articles 27 to 34 of Section 5 of Part II set out the provisions relating to patents. These are minimum standards. Members of the World Trade Organisation may under their domestic laws give enhanced protection but must ensure that these minimum standards are met. Part III sets out the provisions for enforcing rights including civil and administrative procedures and remedies. Part IV sets out the requirements and principles for obtaining and maintaining intellectual property rights and related *inter partes* proceedings.

Hong Kong is a founding member in its own right of the World Trade Organisation. The *Intellectual Property (World Trade Organisation Amendments) Ordinance* was enacted in April 1996. This was an interim arrangement to harmonise current intellectual property laws with the TRIPs Agreement. As indicated above, s 11 of the *Intellectual Property (World Trade Organisation Amendments) Ordinance* amended ss 7A to 7D of the *Registration of Patents Ordinance* to bring the government use provisions in line with the TRIPs Agreement.

Proposed Patent Law Treaty

Proposals for a new international treaty dealing with patents have been discussed within the World Intellectual Property Organisation for a number of years. Eleven meetings of a Committee of Experts on the Harmonisation of certain Provisions in Laws for the Protection of Inventions were held between 1984 and 1991.[5] The first part of a Diplomatic Conference for the Conclusion of a Treaty Supplementing the Paris Convention as far as Patents are Concerned was held in the Hague in 1991, based on the work of the Committee of Experts. This Conference did not result in a new patent law treaty although, in many areas, consensus was reached.

In 1994 a further Committee of Experts was set up by the World Intellectual Property Organisation to consider a patent law treaty dealing with procedural aspects for obtaining and maintaining patents. Many of these issues had been considered in the earlier discussions and it was noted that the Trademark Law Treaty concluded in 1994 dealt with similar procedural aspects in respect of trademark law. A number of meetings of the Committee of Experts have been held but as yet no diplomatic conference to bring this into effect has been held.

The purpose of the current proposals for a patent law treaty is to provide harmonised procedures worldwide in areas relating to applications for a patent and renewing and maintaining a patent. The new law takes account of these harmonisation proposals, in so far as is possible, for a registration system where application in the first instance is made to another patent office.

Summary of Factors for Change

Deficiencies in the old law, the change of sovereignty on 1 July 1997, international developments with the advent of the TRIPs Agreement and patent law discussions within the World Intellectual Property Organisation, have all been important factors in the impetus for change to Hong Kong's patent system.

Steering Committee

In 1987 the Attorney General and the Financial Secretary of the Hong Kong Government set up a Patent Steering Committee[6] to advise as stated in para 2.2 of the report '... in the light of responses already received, on what patent system should be adopted in Hong Kong and, to draw up detailed proposals for the implementation of the system'. The Committee comprised professionals in the patent field in Hong Kong and included representatives from the Hong Kong Government.

The Patents Steering Committee completed its report in January 1993 and it was published and issued for consultation by the Hong Kong Government in May 1993.

The deliberations of the Patents Steering Committee coincided with a period of intense activity and discussion in respect of intellectual property in international fora. As mentioned above, discussions for a proposed patent law treaty were taking place under the auspices of the World Intellectual Property Organisation. The period from 1989 to 1993, in particular, saw continued expansion of the countries adhering to the Paris Convention and the PCT. The Uruguay Round of the General Agreement on Tariffs and Trade was in progress. It was during the early stages of the Uruguay Round discussions that it was agreed to add intellectual property to the subjects for agreement during this Round. The conclusion of the Uruguay Round saw the establishment of the World Trade Organisation and the Agreement on Trade Related Aspects of Intellectual Property. The content of what was to become the TRIPs Agreement was substantially finalised in late 1992, particularly as it related to patents.

Patents Steering Committee Report

Content

The Patents Steering Committee Report was comprehensive. It contained 15 Chapters and two annexures. Chapters 3-15 contained the substance of the report and dealt with the following:

Chapter 3	General introduction to patents
Chapter 4	Patent systems
Chapter 5	Patent systems – registering patents granted elsewhere
Chapter 6	Hong Kong's present legal system for protecting patents
Chapter 7	Trade and economic issues
Chapter 8	Trade, economic and legal constraints on change
Chapter 9	Recommended patent system
Chapter 10	Part I Proposals for a Patents Bill
	Part II Outline of Proposals for a Patents Bill
Chapter 11	Does Hong Kong need a petty patent system?
Chapter 12	Options for a petty patent system

Chapter 13	Part I Recommended petty patent system Part II Proposals for petty patents in the Patents Bill
Chapter 14	International conventions and organisations
Chapter 15	Technical information

Overall recommendations

In summary the Patents Steering Committee's recommendations can be broadly defined as follows:

- Hong Kong should have its own independent patent system based on the registration of patents granted elsewhere;
- The patent system should incorporate provisions for the grant of a short-term or petty patent to protect inventions with a short term commercial life; and
- A technical information centre should be set up to provide improved technical information and skilled assistance in accessing such information.

Patents

Chapters 4-8 of the Patents Steering Committee Report considered options for the patent system and the factors affecting any proposals for change. Chapter 9 contained the recommendations taking all factors into account. Chapter 10 contained the proposals for a Patents Bill.

In Chapters 4 and 5, the Patents Steering Committee considered the options for the new system. These can be divided into five categories:

1. Original application and grant in Hong Kong with full search and examination before grant (examination system);
2. Original application and grant in Hong Kong without search and examination before grant (non-examination system);
3. Original grant with search and examination contracted out to another patent office;
4. Original grant using the PCT; and
5. Application in Hong Kong based on the registration of patents granted elsewhere (registration system).

The first of these options, namely search and examination carried out in Hong Kong, was rejected. It was considered unjustified for Hong

Kong to set up its own search and examination system in view of the substantial investment in personnel and other resources required and the time it would take to acquire search and examination expertise.

The second option, a non-examination system, was also rejected on the basis that this would not give Hong Kong a strong, well-respected patent system. The advantages of an examination system are many but, in particular, a patent granted after search and examination does give a degree of certainty to patent proprietors and can avoid abuse by the proprietor of the monopoly right given by the patent.

The third and fourth options were rejected on the basis that even if search and examination was carried out by another patent office, whether as part of the PCT or by contracting out, some assessment as to patentability in Hong Kong would still be required before the patent was granted. This would also require investment in resources, particularly skilled personnel.

The final option of a registration system was considered in depth in Chapter 5. The Patents Steering Committee considered that the main advantage of a registration system was that it could provide a cost effective patent system for Hong Kong. From the patent proprietor's perspective, it has the advantage of being simpler and less expensive to obtain than an original grant. This is particularly so where the proprietor wishes to obtain a patent in that place as well as Hong Kong. A perceived disadvantage is that the owner of an invention cannot apply initially in Hong Kong. An application must be made elsewhere first. However, if such an owner also wants a patent in such other place then this is less a disadvantage than may seem at first.

The options for a registration system, as identified by the Patents Steering Committee, fell into the following categories, namely, to register

- patents granted by any patent office;
- patents granted by patent offices which granted patents after full search and examination before grant; and
- patents granted by a single or selected patent offices.

The Patents Steering Committee rejected the first two options in view of the differences in the scope and quality of patents granted by different patent offices. In considering the last option, the Patents

Steering Committee noted the patent systems of various countries and jurisdictions.

In assessing the various systems it was considered that any system on which registration was based should at least have

- a high level of trade with Hong Kong;
- a high number of patents with an international spread of applicants;
- the same standards and ambit of protection as currently applied in Hong Kong; and
- use the English language.

The Patents Steering Committee considered but rejected the option of registering patents from the United States Trademark and Patent Office, and the Japanese Patent Office.

The United States is one of Hong Kong's major trading partners and the United States Trademark and Patent Office has a large number of patents and deals with a broad range of applicants. However, it was considered that the differences between the United States patent law and Hong Kong's old law and the need for continuity with the existing system precluded the option of registering United States patents. The Patents Steering Committee Report noted that the current law is based on the principle of first-to-file, which differs substantially from United States patent law, which is based on the principle of first-to-invent.

As far as the Japanese Patent Office was concerned, the major stumbling block was the question of language. The Patents Steering Committee considered that English should be the primary language and that any patent system should use English as a primary language to avoid the need for expensive translations.

The Patents Steering Committee considered that the European Patent Office appeared to satisfy all the criteria. It receives a large number and wide range of patents. The countries that form the European Patent Convention are major trading partners with Hong Kong. The European Patent Convention provided a patent law that was the same as the Hong Kong patent system.

The Patents Steering Committee also considered the changes taking place in Chinese patent law, which would make the system more compatible with Hong Kong patent law, and the proposal that China would join the PCT in 1994. China is Hong Kong's major trading partner and although the number of patent applications received by the Chinese Patent Office was relatively low at the time, the Committee took note of the special relationship with Hong Kong.

The Patents Steering Committee Report set out the Committee's concerns regarding the registration of patents from more than one system, but considered that in certain circumstances these difficulties could be overcome.

The patent law recommendations in Chapter 9[7] were in essence as follows:

- Hong Kong should have its own patent law and administrative system for patents;
- The patent law should provide for the grant of an independent patent based on the registration of patents granted by the European Patent Office and in the second phase, the Chinese Patent Office; and
- The patent when granted should be independent of the patent granted in the original patent office and be capable of being tested for validity and infringement, rectified or revoked according to the patent law of Hong Kong, independent of action taken elsewhere.

Petty patents (short-term patents)

Chapters 11 and 12 of the Patents Steering Committee Report considered the need for a petty patent system and the options for such a system. The basic concept of a petty patent or a short-term patent as it is referred to in the *Patents Ordinance*, is that it should fill a perceived shortcoming in the protection available for certain types of inventions. The mainstream patent system, which provides for a patent granted after full search and examination and for a term of 20 years, benefits, in the main, those patent owners who see a long-term financial return from their patent. The Patents Steering Committee, however, identified the fact that those business people whose inventions have only a short-term commercial life may find that the expense and time involved in obtaining such a patent is not warranted. Such inventions may thus be unprotected in practice, even though in all other respects they fulfil the necessary criteria for patentability.

The Patents Steering Committee considered whether Hong Kong needed such an addition to the patent system and then weighed up the various options. By a majority only, the Patents Steering Committee recommended that Hong Kong should introduce a petty patent system. They recommended a non-examination system with certain special modifications to avoid potential abuse of the system.

In particular, they recommended that a search report should be filed before grant and that, where an interlocutory injunction was ordered, both parties should have a right to call for a speedy trial. The Patents Steering Committee recommended that the standards for the patenting of inventions should be the same for both patents and petty patents. The minority view in the Patents Steering Committee Report was that the system proposed would lead to uncertainty and give considerable scope for abuse.

Model bill

In accordance with the terms of reference, the Patents Steering Committee Report contained a model Patents Bill in Chapters 10 and 13, which fleshed out in detail the patent and petty patent law proposals. After considering relevant legislation, the Patents Steering Committee based the model Patents Bill on the United Kingdom *Patents Act* 1977, but in some areas followed more closely the European Patent Convention. The *Patents Act* 1977 is framed so as to have as nearly as practicable the same effect as the corresponding provisions of the European Patent Convention and the Community Patent Convention.[8] The Chinese Patent Law has many aspects in common with the European Patent Convention, particularly as regards patentability.

Technical Information Centre

In Chapter 15, the Patents Steering Committee considered the need for a technical information centre in Hong Kong. They recommended the establishment in Hong Kong of a technical information centre providing services similar to those provided by a number of patent offices and technical information organisations worldwide. The Committee recognised that it might be necessary, initially, to tailor the technical information to Hong Kong's specific requirements given the vast body of available technical information and the costs involved. They recommended conducting a survey of these requirements.

Consultation on the Patents Steering Committee's Recommendation

Consultation

The Patents Steering Committee Report was issued for consultation in Hong Kong to a broad range of consultees. According to the Hong Kong Government, the Committee proposals received broad support. They are now reflected in the *Patents Ordinance*. The draft Patents Bill was also circulated among the original consultees. Certain changes were made before the Bill was published in the Hong Kong Government Gazette.

Consideration of the Recommendations

The patent system

The Committee's proposals were designed to provide an independent well-respected and strong patent system which was cost-effective and in line with international standards.

Two aspects require special mention because they are likely to continue to be important to users of the system and should be kept in mind if there are to be any changes to the patent system in future.

The first of these was the emphasis on an evolutionary approach to ensure continuity with the current system. This reflects the importance, in this complex area, of continued access to an established body of case law – for the benefit of both users and the judiciary.

The other important consideration was the need to give a choice to inventors and patent proprietors. A registration system is most cost effective if an inventor can use the patent system where the product will be marketed as a base for his patent in Hong Kong, because such person would, in any event, be obtaining a patent there.

Petty patents

There have been many discussions on the issue of petty, short-term or utility model patent systems worldwide. The numbers of jurisdictions providing short-term patent type protection are on the rise and many of these places are providing or changing to non-examination systems.

Unlike the system proposed for Hong Kong, many jurisdictions with petty patent systems limit the subject matter or scope of protection. There are arguments for and against this approach, but, starting as it was from scratch, it seemed sensible for Hong Kong to opt for a short-term patent system which would share the same patentability standards as the main system. The distinction between the inventive step required to be shown before grant of a standard patent and a petty patent is difficult to define and could lead to problems of interpretation.

Concerns expressed in Hong Kong on this issue endorsed the benefits of the proposed system, but also mirrored the concerns expressed by the minority view in the Patents Steering Committee Report.

Technical Information Centre

The concept of setting up such a centre or centres has not been taken forward as yet. The philosophy set out in the Patents Steering Committee Report is that facilities should be made available to provide both patent and non-patent information to users and to assist access to such information. It is hoped that the Hong Kong Government, in conjunction with industry and academic institutions in Hong Kong, will exploit new technologies such as CD-ROM and the Internet to provide wider and better access to this information.

The Committee also recommended that Hong Kong patent information should be made available in electronic form. Approval for a Patents Registry computer system that would allow for this was given in July 1996.

New Law

Proposals

The *Patents Ordinance* (No 52 of 1997) was enacted on 28 May 1997 and reflects, in the main, the proposals of the Patents Steering Committee. In particular it provides for the grant of an independent patent based on the registration of patents granted by designated patent offices. The patent, once granted, will be independent of the patent granted by the designated patent office. The patent will be enforced in Hong Kong and, apart from some minor exceptions, this will be irrespective of action taken in any other jurisdiction. The Ordinance also provides for the grant of a short-term patent and contains provisions which enable the patent and short-term patent to be tested for validity, enforced, rectified and amended in Hong Kong.

Designated Patent Offices

The patent offices designated for the purposes of the new law are

- the United Kingdom Patent Office;
- the European Patent Office in respect of patents designating the United Kingdom; and
- the Chinese Patent Office.

The Sino-British Joint Liaison Group agreed to proposals for the new law. Provisions allowing for registration of these three types of patent took effect with the commencement of the new law and continue after 1 July 1997.

It is understood that after a suitable period of time there will be a gradual transition to a system based on the registration of patents from the Chinese Patent Office alone. However, the timing and manner of phasing out of United Kingdom and European Patent Office patents and provisions for the continued protection for these patents would be for the future Hong Kong Special Administrative Region Government to decide. The new law contains no provision for this phasing out.

Patents Ordinance

The Patents Bill was introduced to the Legislative Council on the 10 July 1996 and was enacted as the *Patents Ordinance* on 28 May 1997. A Bills Committee of the Legislative Council, which held 11 meetings, considered the Bill.

As a result of the deliberations a number of changes were made to the Bill by way of Committee Stage amendments. These amendments amounted to simple drafting changes in some cases and to substantial policy changes in others. The major concerns addressed by the Bills Committee and the changes made were highlighted by the Secretary for Trade and Industry when moving for the resumption of the Second Reading of the Bill.

The major changes and concerns are outlined below:

- Clause 73(2) of the Patents Bill provided that 'goods in transit' were not considered to be an 'import' for the purposes of s 73 (1) and were thus not protected. As a result of submissions from the legal profession it was decided to remove Clause 73(2) and leave the question to be developed by the common law and the courts.
- Provisions allowing for interlocutory injunctions for short-term patents concerned the Bills Committee. Following submissions from the legal profession and to remain in line with international norms, no change was made. Subject to the provisions of s 129 of the *Patents Ordinance*, it is possible to obtain interlocutory relief for short-term patents. However, the Hong Kong Government has agreed to review its position one year after introduction of the new law in light of any indications that this form of relief has been abused.
- The Bills Committee expressed concern about the filing requirements for short-term patent applications. It considered that there might be some practical difficulty in filing search reports in support of a short-term patent contemporaneously with the patent application. No change was made as the relevant sections of the Ordinance and Rules allow for time to comply with the formal requirements. A change has made, however, to s 119 of the *Patents Ordinance*, which now provides that the grant of a short-term patent can be deferred for 12 months, rather than 6 months as provided for in the Patents Bill.
- A new provision has been included to provide for the filing of a short-term patent based on an international application under the PCT. Thus s 125 of the *Patents Ordinance* gives an applicant who has made an international application designating a utility model in China the right to make an application for a short-term patent within six months after the international application has entered the national phase in China.

Subsidiary Legislation

The subsidiary legislation will govern administrative arrangements and the transitional provisions.

The Patents (General) Rules

The *Patents (General) Rules* (LN 339 of 1997) made by the Registrar under s 149 of the *Patents Ordinance* set out

- detailed procedural matters;
- the fees;
- the relevant searching authorities which can issue a search report to be filed in support of an application for a short-term patent; and
- the relevant opposition or revocation proceedings in designated patent offices for purposes of ss 43, 44 and 91(1) of the *Patents Ordinance*.

Specified Forms

The Registrar also has the power under s 150 of the *Patents Ordinance* to require the use of certain forms, as published in the Gazette, in proceedings before the Registrar. This is a new departure in that the forms will not form part of the Rules and can as a result be amended more easily to reflect changing requirements and technology. A Notice of Specification of Forms was published in the Gazette on 24 June 1997 (GN3186 of 1997).

Patents (Transitional Arrangements) Rules

The *Patents (Transitional Arrangements) Rules* (LN 335 of 1997) made by the Governor-in-Council under s 157 of the *Patents Ordinance* set out detailed provisions for the continued protection of patents registered and still in force under the existing law. These Transitional Rules will also provide for the grant of patents under the new law in respect of patents granted by the United Kingdom Patent Office before the commencement date and published applications for patents which, if granted, would have been eligible to be registered under the old law.

The Patents (Designation of Patent Offices) Notice

Under s 8 of the *Patents Ordinance* the Governor-in-Council (now the Chief Executive-in-Council) may designate a patent office established under the law of any country or under any international agreement for purposes of the Ordinance. The Patents (Designation of Patent

Offices) Notice was made by the Governor-in-Council and came into effect on 27 June 1997. The Notice designates the Chinese Patent Office, the European Patent Office in respect of patents designating the United Kingdom and the United Kingdom Patent Office as designated patent offices for purposes of the Ordinance.

Commencement date

The *Patents Ordinance* came into force on 27 June 1997 – the date appointed by the Secretary of Trade and Industry.

Summary

A historical summary of the events leading up to the new patent system is set out below:

- Patents Steering Committee appointed in January 1987.
- Patents Steering Committee Report issued for consultation in May 1993.
- Draft Patents Bill issued for consultation in March 1996.
- Patents Bill introduced into the Legislative Council on 10 July 1996.
- Approval by the Finance Committee of a computer system for the administration of the patent system in July 1996.
- *Patents Ordinance* enacted by the Legislative Council after deliberation by the Bills Committee on 24 May 1997.
- Notice of the commencement date of 27 June 1997 given by the Secretary of Trade and Industry under s 1(2) of the *Patents Ordinance.*
- Patents (Designation of Patent Offices) Notice made by the Governor-in-Council under s 8 of the *Patents Ordinance* designating for purposes of the *Patents Ordinance* the Chinese Patent Office, the European Patent Office in respect of patents designating the United Kingdom and the United Kingdom Patent Office with effect from 27 June 1997.
- *Patents (General) Rules* made by the Registrar under s 149 of the *Patents Ordinance,* which came into operation on the commencement date.

- *Patents (Transitional Arrangements) Rules* made by the Governor-in-Council which came into operation on the commencement date.
- Notice of specification of forms given by the Registrar which came into effect on the commencement date.

The new patent system has had a long gestation period but this reflects not only the complexity of the issues involved, but also international developments over the past ten years. Any changes to the patent system in future should be made with due regard for the reasoning and careful deliberation behind the new law's provisions.

Notes

1 *Canon Kabushiki Kaisha v Green Cartridge Company (Hong Kong) Ltd and Anor* (FSR [1995] p 877).

2 The Joint Declaration of the Government of the United Kingdom of Britain and Northern Ireland and the Government of the People's Republic of China on the Question of Hong Kong.

3 The Basic Law of the Hong Kong Special Administrative Region of the People's Republic of China promulgated and adopted by the National Peoples Congress of the People's Republic of China on 4 April 1990 to be put into effect on 1 July 1997.

4 Speech given by Averil C Waters, Deputy Director of Intellectual Property in November 1995 at a workshop during the 38th Council Meeting of the Asian Patent Attorney's Association, Hong Kong.

5 World Intellectual Property Organization Records of the Diplomatic Conference for the Conclusion of Treaty Supplementing the Paris Convention as far as Patents are Concerned, The Hague,1991.

6 Patent Steering Committee Report dated January 1993 and issued for consultation in May 1993.

7 Patents Steering Committee: paras 9.36 to 9.40.

8 Section 130(7) *Patents Act* 1977.

3 Overview: The Old Patent Law, Patents Ordinance, Patents Rules and Transitional Provisions

Overview of the Old Law

The former patent system in Hong Kong was a registration system that relied on a patent granted by the United Kingdom Patent Office. The patent continued to rely on the United Kingdom system after registration in Hong Kong.

The Current Law

The *Registration of Patents Ordinance* provided for the registration of patents granted under the *Patents Acts* 1949 and 1977 (United Kingdom patents) and European patents designating the United Kingdom which take effect in the United Kingdom, pursuant to the *Patents Act* 1977 (European patents (UK)).[1]

The *Registration of Patents Ordinance* was repealed by s 154 of the *Patents Ordinance*. Certain provisions of the repealed Ordinance relating to the validity of instruments, Crown use and infringement continue to apply in relation to acts done before the commencement date of the new law.

The Old Law in Outline

Application

Application could be made at any time within five years after the grant of patent by the United Kingdom Patent Office. The application had to be accompanied by a certified copy of the specification, a translation if it was published in a language other than English, a certificate issued by the United Kingdom Comptroller giving full particulars of the grant and a statutory declaration setting out the interest and title of the applicant.[2]

Registration

The Registrar had to register the patent and issue the certificate[3] if the formality requirements were complied with.

Term

The patent remained in force so long as it was in force in the United Kingdom. In effect, the term is a period of 20 years from the date of application in the United Kingdom Patent Office or European Patent Office subject to it remaining in force in the United Kingdom.

Renewal

There was no requirement to renew in Hong Kong but the patent had to be renewed in the United Kingdom to remain in force in Hong Kong. There was no requirement to record the fact of renewal in Hong Kong.

Rights

On registration the proprietor had the same rights as if the patent had been granted in the United Kingdom with an extension to Hong Kong. In effect, it has been established by the case law that the proprietor had the right to seek relief in the Hong Kong courts based on the right to bring an infringement action given by the *Patents Act* 1977.[4] These rights continue to apply to acts done before the commencement date by virtue of s 157 of the *Patents Ordinance*.

Remedies

The proprietor could bring infringement action and had the right to seek the normal common law remedies of injunction, an order to deliver up and damages.

Amendment of the specification

The courts in Hong Kong could not amend the specification, but a proprietor could record details of any amendment of the specification or drawings made according to the United Kingdom law.[5]

Revocation

The patent could not be revoked in Hong Kong. On revocation in the United Kingdom the patent was no longer in force and accordingly was not protected in Hong Kong. There was no mechanism to record any such revocation in the Hong Kong Patents Registry. Under the transitional provisions, patents no longer in force on the commencement date will not be transferred to the new register.

Registration of assignments, transmissions and other transactions

Assignments, transmissions and other transactions could be recorded in the Hong Kong Patents Registry on making an application, supported by a statutory declaration and original or certified copies of supporting documents.[6]

Government use

If the Governor-in-Council declared a period of extreme urgency, any person duly authorised by the Governor had the right to use the invention without the consent of the proprietor. The proprietor was to be notified of such government use and receive reasonable remuneration. Any dispute with regard to such government use could be referred to the court.[7]

The Register and search facilities

The Hong Kong Patents Registry maintained a register giving details of the proprietor, the title of the invention and other relevant data. The patent specification could be inspected but the file maintained by the Registrar was not open to inspection. The Register and search facilities were manually based.

Overview of the Patents Ordinance

The *Patents Ordinance* is divided into a total of 19 parts (Parts I to XIX) and 2 Schedules. It provides for the grant of a patent (called a standard patent in the Ordinance) based on the registration of patents granted by a designated patent office for a term of 20 years, subject to renewal. It also provides for the grant of a short-term patent after original application in Hong Kong for a term of eight years, subject to renewal. The Ordinance sets out the provisions that enable the standard patent and the short-term patent to be tested for validity, enforced, rectified, revoked and amended in Hong Kong. In the Ordinance the term *patent* is defined to include both a standard patent and a short-term patent.

The Patents Ordinance in Outline

Part	Description and Content
Part I	**Preliminary** Part I (**ss 1 to 9**) sets out the general interpretation provisions and certain other provisions including the power of the Chief Executive-in-Council to designate a designated patent office for the purposes of the new law.
Part II	**Applications for Standard Patents** Part II (**ss 10 to 30**) deals with the application for and the grant of a standard patent and provides for grant of a standard patent based on the registration of patents granted by a designated patent office. It sets out the two-stage application procedure and provides for filing of a request to record the designated patent application[8] in the first stage and request to register the designated patent[9] and for grant of the standard patent in the second stage. This Part provides for the request to record to be entered on the register and published and the standard patent to be granted and published after the formal requirements are complied with.
Part III	**Provisions as to Applications for a Standard Patent before Grant** Part III (**ss 31 to 37**) deals with certain aspects of the application that arise before grant including amendment, withdrawal and maintenance of the application and the right of the Registrar to refuse to register the request to record if the application is contrary to *ordre public*.

Part	Description and Content
Part IV	**Provisions as to Patents after Grant** Part IV (**ss 38 to 49**) deals with certain aspects of the standard and short-term patent after grant, including amendment of the specification on application to the court. It deals with the deemed date of filing, term, and the renewal and restoration of a standard patent. This Part also contains special provisions for amending and revoking a standard patent after amendment or revocation of the corresponding designated patent in prescribed opposition or rectification proceedings in the relevant designated patent office.
Part V	**Property in Patents and Applications; Registration** Part V (**ss 50 to 56**) deals with the nature of and transactions in, patents and patent applications, the effect of registration of transactions and provides for the maintenance of the register. It also provides for the making of rules requiring the registration of transactions, instruments or events affecting rights in patents or applications for standard patents.
Part VI	**Employees' Inventions** Part VI (**ss 57 to 61**) deals with the question of employees' inventions and the right of compensation for employees for certain inventions on application to the court. This Part applies only to inventions made after the commencement date and to employees who, at the time the invention was made, were mainly employed in Hong Kong or, if the employees' place of business could not be determined, whose employer had a place of business in Hong Kong.
Part VII	**Contracts as to Patented Products and Other Aspects** Part VII (**ss 62 to 63**) deals with certain aspects of contracts relating *inter alia* to the supply or licence of patented products.
Part VIII	**Compulsory Licences for Standard Patents** Part VIII (**ss 64 to 67**) contains provisions for the grant, on application to the court, of a compulsory licence for a standard patent at any time after the expiration of three years following grant of the standard patent. This sets out the grounds on which application can be made and the basis on which the court should grant such a licence.
Part IX	**Government Use of Patented Inventions** Part IX (**ss 68 to 72**) deals with government use of patented inventions after a declaration of extreme urgency made by the Chief Executive-in-Council

Part	Description and Content
Part X	**Effects of Patent and Patent Application** Part X (**ss 73 to 79**) sets out the rights of the proprietor of a patent granted under the *Patents Ordinance.*
Part XI	**Infringement** Part XI (**ss 80 to 90**) sets out the remedies for infringement of a patent and the rights on publication of the application for a standard patent. It also contains a remedy for threats of groundless infringement proceedings.
Part XII	**Revocation of Patents** Part XII (**ss 91 to 101**) contains general provisions related to the revocation of a patent on application to the court, provisions as to patentability of a patent, the question of priority of a standard patent, the right to a patent and proceedings in which validity can be disputed.
Part XIII	**General Provisions as to Amendment of Patents and Patent Applications** Part XIII (**ss 102 to 103**) deals with amendments to patent specifications and patent applications and provides for such amendments to be invalid to the extent that they include added matter.
Part XIV	**Language of the Proceedings and Authentic Text** Part XIV (**ss 104 to 107**) provides that an application must be filed in one of the official languages, ie English or Chinese, and contains provisions dealing with the language of proceedings and establishing the language of the authentic text.
Part XV	**Short-term Patents** Part XV (**ss 108 to 129**) contains the special provisions relating to short-term patents. It deals with the pre-grant aspects, including the right to claim priority for a short-term patent under the Paris Convention, the application procedures and grant. It also contains provisions for making an application based on an international application. This Part provides for the term, renewal and restoration of a short-term patent and contains special provisions relating to court proceedings.
Part XVI	**Miscellaneous** Part XVI (**ss 130 to 140**) deals with appeals from decisions of the Registrar and other matters relating to procedural aspects of proceedings before the Registrar or the court. It also provides for the reversal of the burden of proof in such proceedings in respect of patented processes for obtaining new products.

Part	Description and Content
Part XVII	**Offences** Part XVII (**ss 141 to 145**) provides for certain offences, including the offences of falsifying the Register and making unauthorised claims of patent rights or patent applications.
Part XVIII	**Administrative Provisions** Part XVIII (**ss 146 to 153**) contains certain administrative provisions and, in particular, provides for the inspection of patent applications and patents and for the inspection of documents. This Part also authorises the Registrar to make rules, specify forms and generally regulate practice and procedure under the *Patents Ordinance.*
Part XIX	**Repeals and Transitional Arrangements** Part XIX (**ss 154 to 163**) provides for the repeal of the *Registration of Patents Ordinance*, sets out certain of the transitional arrangements and gives the Chief Executive-in-Council the power to make rules dealing with the remainder of the transitional arrangements. This Part also includes consequential amendments made to other Ordinances.
Schedule 1	**Convention Countries and World Trade Organisation Members** Schedule 1 sets out the countries that have acceded to the Paris Convention and the members of the World Trade Organisation.
Schedule 2	**Registration of Patents Ordinance** Schedule 2 sets out the provisions of s 7G of the *Registration of Patents Ordinance,* as amended.

Patents (General) Rules in Outline

The *Patents (General) Rules* are divided into fifteen Parts and three Schedules. The purpose of the Rules is to provide for the procedures to be followed under the *Patents Ordinance* in relation to making applications for patents and other proceedings. The *Patents (General) Rules* are subsidiary legislation made by the Registrar under s 149 of the *Patents Ordinance*.

Part	Description and Content
Part I	**Preliminary** Part I (ss 1 to 2) sets out the general interpretation provisions in the Rules and also provides that the Rules will come into operation on the same date as the *Patents Ordinance*.
Part II	**Applications for Standard Patents** Part II (ss 3 to 26) deals with the procedures for the application and grant of a standard patent and related proceedings. It sets out the procedures for making a reference to the Registrar on who has a right to apply and for the making of orders following from such a reference. It sets out the specific requirements and content of the request to record a designated patent application and the request for registration and grant. It also sets out the specific requirements and contents of documents to be filed in support including the presentation of documents and the date of publication of the designated patent application for the purpose of filing an application which is based on an international application. This Part sets out the provisions for making good any deficiencies in the documents making up the request to record and the request to register and grant of the standard patent, including making an application for restoration of rights. It also provides for the detail of making a request to record a divisional application.
Part III	**Provisions as to Application for A Standard Patent before Grant** Part III (ss 27 to 31) sets out the procedures dealing with certain aspects of the application which arise before grant including amendment and maintenance of the application.
Part IV	**Provisions as to Patents after Grant** Part IV (ss 32 to 41) sets out the procedures dealing with certain aspects of the standard and short-term patent after grant, ie the procedures for renewal and restoration of standard patents, the amendment and revocation of a standard patent under ss 43 and 44 of the *Patents Ordinance* and procedures for an inventor to apply to the Registrar for a finding that he is entitled to be mentioned in the patent as the inventor. This Part sets out the prescribed opposition or revocation proceedings for the purposes of ss 43 and 44 of the *Patents Ordinance*. This Part also sets out the requirements and procedures for filing with the Registrar the relevant particulars when the court orders an amendment of the patent, on surrender of a patent and on making a reference to the Registrar to revoke a patent on grounds of '*ordre public*' or morality .

Part	Description and Content
Part V	**Property in Patents and Applications; Registration** Part V (ss 42 to 52) sets out the procedures dealing with transactions in patents, applications for a patent and other related matters including the procedures for registering an address for service, the alteration of name or address, transactions, instruments or events affecting rights in patents or applications for standard patents and requests for correction of errors. This Part sets the procedures for inspecting the register and obtaining certificates and copies of the entries on the register and the requirements for filing of orders or directions given by the court in relation to a patent or application.
Part VI	**Employees' Inventions** Part VI (s 53) sets the time limit prescribed by s 53 in which an application for compensation can be made to the court by an employee.
Part VII	**Revocation of Patents** Part VII (ss 54 to 55) sets out the prescribed opposition or revocation proceedings in a designated patent office for the purposes of the revocation of a standard patent under s 91(1)(i) of the *Patents Ordinance* and sets out the prescribed exhibition or meetings for the purposes of s 95(1)(b) of the *Patents Ordinance*.
Part VIII	**Language of the Proceedings; Authentic Text** Part VIII (ss 56 to 57) sets out the requirements for filing translations of documents or parts of those documents which are not in one of the official languages; the information to be supplied in both official languages; the language to be used in oral proceedings; and the requirements for filing a corrected translation.
Part IX	**Short-term Patents** Part IX (ss 58 to 74) sets out the procedures and requirements for making an application for a short-term patent and for making a divisional short-term patent application. It sets out the requirements for the content of the application including the description, drawings, abstract and claims, and the size and presentation of documents. It sets out the procedures required where the applicant is not the inventor, for claiming priority for a short-term patent under the Paris Convention and for making a claim regarding a non-prejudicial disclosure. This Part also sets out the provisions for making good any deficiencies in the documents making up the short-term patent application. It also prescribes the Searching Authorities, sets out the requirements for the content of the search report, and refers to Schedule 1 which sets out the requirements concerning applications relating to micro-organisms.

Part	Description and Content
Part X	**Procedure Up To and Including Grant of Short-term Patents** Part X (ss 75 to 78) sets out the procedures on amendment, reinstatement and restoration of rights of an application for a short-term patent and provides for the alternate date for the purposes of a short-term patent application based on an international application.
Part XI	**Provisions as to Short-term Patents after Grant** Part XI (ss 79 to 81) sets out the procedures for renewal of short-term patents and restoration of lapsed short-term patents.
Part XII	**Hearings and Agents** Part XII (ss 82 to 87) sets out the procedures for the hearing of a person adversely affected by the exercise of a discretion by the Registrar. This Part also sets out the requirements where a document is to be signed by partnerships, companies and associations and in respect of acts done by an agent. It also contains matters relating to the award of costs and the giving of security for costs.
Part XIII	**Information and Inspection** Part XIII (ss 88 to 92) sets out the cases where information relating to a standard patent or standard patent application can be made available and the restrictions on documents which can be inspected as well as the procedures and requirements in relation to confidential documents.
Part XIV	**Miscellaneous** Part XIV (ss 93 to 104) sets out the requirements in relation to the service of documents, the correction of irregularities, dispensation with certain requirements by the Registrar, evidence and making of statutory declarations and affidavits, and the verification of documents. It also gives the power to the Registrar to make directions and appoint advisers, to publish and sell certain documents and to publish and advertise information filed under the Ordinance. This part gives the Registrar the power to extend the time periods prescribed by the Rules other than those specified. This Part and Schedule 2 provides for the fees to be paid in relation to applications and proceedings under the Ordinance.

Part	Description and Content
Part XV	**Transitional** Part XV (ss 105 to 112) sets out the requirements for entries in the register in relation to standard patents granted or deemed to be granted under the *Patents (Transitional Arrangements) Rules*. This Part also sets out the procedures for any deletion from the register of the particulars of a deemed standard patent, request for information relating to patents granted under the *Registration of Patents Ordinance* and the modification of the *Patents (General) Rules* in relation to applications for a standard patent under the *Patents (Transitional Arrangements) Rules*.
Schedule 1	**Micro-organisms** This Schedule sets out the procedures and requirements when an invention which is the subject of an application for a short-term patent, or a short-term patent, requires for its performance the use of a micro-organism.
Schedule 2	**Fees** This Schedule sets out the fees for matters and proceedings under the *Patents Ordinance*.
Schedule 3	**Modified Application of the Patents (General) Rules to Applications for Standard Patents by Virtue of the Transitional Rules** Parts I and II of this Schedule sets out those parts of the *Patents (General) Rules* which are modified for making applications for a standard patent under the *Patents (Transitional Arrangements) Rules*.

Specified Forms

Under s 150 of the *Patents Ordinance* the Registrar has the power to specify those forms which are required to be used in connection with any proceedings under the *Patents Ordinance*. This is done by giving notice of these forms in the Hong Kong Government Gazette. This means that forms can be easily changed if this is required as a result of practical or technical requirements. It is, of course, not necessary for the actual printed forms to be used.

The forms which were notified in the Hong Kong Government Gazette on 24 June 1997 and which came into effect on 27 June 1997 are listed below.

Form No	**Title of Form**	**Patents Ordinance**	**Patents (General) Rules**	**Patents (Transitional Arrangements) Rules**
Patents Form P1 Version 06.97	On reference to the Registrar for determination before grant in respect of questions as to • who is entitled to apply for grant of standard patent; and • entitlement of grant of a licence or whether the periods or terms of such licence are reasonable.	s 13 and 14	ss 3, 4, 7	
Patents Form P2 Version 06.97	Filing of notice of opposition or counter-statement in duplicate.	ss 13, 14, 44, 45, 48, 49, 146	ss 3, 4, 7, 37, 38, 40, 41, 48, 108	s 13
Patents Form P3 Version 06.97	Application for authorization by the Registrar.	s 13(5)	s 6	
Patents Form P4 Version 06.97	Request to record a designated patent application for a standard patent.	ss 15, 16, 22	ss 8, 18	
Patents FormP4A (TR) Version 06.97	Request to record a designated patent application for a standard patent by virtue of s 7 *Patents (Transitional Arrangements) Rules*.			s 7
Patents Form P5 Version 06.97	Request for registration of a designated patent and grant of a standard patent.	s 23	s 29	
Patents Form P5A (TR) Version 06.97	Request for registration of a designated patent application and grant of a standard patent by virtue of ss 6, 7, 8, 9 *Patents (Transitional Arrangements) Rules*.			ss 6, 7, 8, 9

Form No	Title of Form	Patents Ordinance	Patents (General) Rules	Patents (Transitional Arrangements) Rules
Patents Form P6 Version 06.97	Request for grant of a short-term patent .	ss 113, 116, 125	ss 58, 74	
Patents Form P7 Version 06.97	Statement of inventorship in respect of a short-term patent.	s 113	s 65	
Patents Form P8 Version 06.97	Request to make an amendment.	s 31, 43, 46, 120	ss 27, 35, 36, 39, 75	
Patents Form P9 Version 06.97	Maintaining application for standard patent (and additional fee for late payment).	s 33	s 28	
Patents Form P10 Version 06.97	Request for renewal of standard patent (and additional fee for late payment).	s 39	s 32	
Patents Form P11 Version 06.97	Request for renewal of a short-term patent (and additional fee for late payment).	s 126	s 79	
Patents Form P12 Version 06.97	Application to restore a withdrawn standard patent application due to non-payment of maintenance fee. Application to restore a lapsed standard patent. Application to restore a lapsed short-term patent.	s 34 s 40 s 127	s 31 s 34 s 81	
Patents Form P13 Version 06.97	Notice requesting reinstatement of a patent application. Application for restoration of rights.	s 28, 123 s 29, 123	s 25, 76 s 26, 77	
Patents Form P14 Version 06.97	Mention of inventor (in duplicate).	s 45	s 38	

Form No	Title of Form	Patents Ordinance	Patents (General) Rules	Patents (Transitional Arrangements) Rules
Patents Form P15 Version 06.97	Filing of notice of revocation of a standard patent. Application for revocation of a standard patent (in duplicate). On reference to the Registrar	s 44 s 44 s 49	ss 36, 37 s 36, 37 s 41	
Patents Form P16 Version 06.97	Notice of offer to surrender a patent.	s 48	s 40	
Patents Form P17 Version 06.97	Notice of appointment or change of agent.		s 85	
Patents Form P18 Version 06.97	Request for alteration of name/address/address for service. Request for correction of address/address for service.		s 45	
Patents Form P19 Version 06.97	Application for registration or notice to the Registrar of rights acquired in or under a patent or a patent application.	ss 50, 51, 52	s 46	
Patents Form P20 Version 06.97	Request for correction of error.	ss 51, 146	ss 47, 48	
Patents Form P21 Version 06.97	Request for information from published standard patent applications or granted patents.	s 147	ss 88, 110	
Patents Form P22 Version 06.97	Request to publish a corrected translation.	s 106	s 57	

Form No	Title of Form	Patents Ordinance	Patents (General) Rules	Patents (Transitional Arrangements) Rules
Patents Form P23	Request for a certified copy of an entry in the register. Request for a certified extract from the register. Request for a certificate for the purposes of s 51(10). Request for a certified copy of a document, specification of a patent or a published standard patent application. Request for a certified extract from a document, specification of a patent or a published standard patent application.	s 51	s 51	
Patents Form P24 Version 06.97	Request for the furnishing of a sample of a deposited micro-organism and notice of confirmation by the Registrar (in quadruplicate).	s 128	s 73	
Patents Form P25 Version 06.97	Application for addition of details in relation to a deemed standard patent to the register. Application for deletion of details in relation to a deemed standard patent from the register.		s 109 s 108	s 13 s 13

Notes

1 Section 2 *Registration of Patents Ordinance*.

2 Sections 3 and 4 *Registration of Patents Ordinance*. See Chapter 2.

3 Sections 5, 6 and 7 *Registration of Patents Ordinance*. See Chapter 2.

4 Section 6 *Registration of Patents Ordinance*. See Chapter 2.

5 Section 9 *Registration of Patents Ordinance*. See Chapter 2.

6 Section 10 *Registration of Patents Ordinance*. See Chapter 2.

7 Sections 7A to 7D *Registration of Patents Ordinance* as amended. See Chapter 2.

8 Designated patent application is defined in s 2 as being a published application for a patent in the designated patent office.

9 Designated patent is defined in s 2 as being a patent granted by a designated patent office.

4 The New Patent Law

This chapter contains an outline of the new law. It explains in brief the proposed new system and the proposed legislation to bring this into effect. It then deals with the main aspects of the new law in outline under separate headings

The proposed new patent system will be a registration system based on the registration of patents granted by a designated patent office for the main or standard patent and a modified non-examination system for the short-term patent.

The grant of a standard patent will be based on the registration of a patent granted by a designated patent office, which carries out full search and examination before grant. A standard patent will be granted after compliance with the formality requirements. After grant, however, the standard patent will be independent of the corresponding designated patent on which it was based.

The short-term patent system will be a non-examination system and the short-term patent will be granted on compliance with the formality requirements.

Both the standard and short-term patent will be capable of being tested for validity and enforced, revoked and amended in Hong Kong under the provisions of the new law. The *Patents Ordinance* has been modelled on the United Kingdom *Patents Act 1977*, which ensures continuity with the existing law.

The New Law

The *Patents Ordinance* provides for the grant of a standard patent on application to the Hong Kong Patents Registry. The grant of patent is based on the registration of a patent granted by a designated patent office and, for the grant of a short-term patent, on original application to the Hong Kong Patents Registry – in both cases after a formality examination only.

Designated Patent Offices

The Chief Executive-in-Council may designate a patent office for the purposes of the new law.[1] The Patents (Designation of Patent Offices) Notice designated the Chinese Patent Office, the European Patent Office in respect of European patents designating the United Kingdom, and the United Kingdom Patent Office for the purposes of the Ordinance with effect from 27 June 1997.

An application based on a patent granted by a designated patent office may only be made where the designated patent application has been published by the designated patent office after the designation of the relevant designated patent office or the commencement date, whichever is the later.[2]

New Law in Outline

Application for a standard patent

An application for a standard patent is a two-stage procedure in Hong Kong. Application for a patent is made, in the first instance, to the designated patent office. At the first stage, application for a standard patent in Hong Kong is made to the Hong Kong Patents Registry within six months of publication of the application by the designated patent office. The second stage of the application is made within six months of the grant of the patent by the designated patent office. Both stages of the application procedure must be complied with to obtain a standard patent.

Application at the first stage is made by filing an application for a request to record the designated patent application.[3] A filing date will be accorded after the minimum requirements are complied with. After a formality check the Registrar will record and publish the request in the register and advertise notice of the grant in the Gazette. Once the request to record is published it is considered to be a published application for a patent.[4]

Application at the second stage is made by filing an application to request to register the corresponding designated patent and to grant the standard patent.[5] A filing date will be accorded after minimum requirements are complied with. After the formalities are complied with the Registrar will register the designated patent and grant the standard patent, publish it and advertise notice of the grant in the Gazette.

The Registrar is required only to ensure that the formal requirements of the application procedure are complied with.[6] The formality procedures follow the methodology used in the European Patent Convention. The Hong Kong Patents Registry will as a first step examine whether the minimum requirements are complied with and if so accord a filing date. Once the filing date is given an examination as to the formal requirements is carried out. Applicants are given time in which to comply with the requirements. The *Patents Rules* provide that applicants will be given a period of two months after notification which can be extended for a further period of two months on application.[7] There are provisions that allow for further processing and restitution of rights in certain circumstances.[8] These formality requirements apply to both stages of the application procedure.

Designated patent application based on an international application under the PCT

There are special provisions to deal with the case where an international application has validly entered into the national phase in the designated patent office. Once such an international application has validly entered the national phase it is considered to be a designated patent application for the purposes of the new law.[9]

The new law provides that application at the first stage must be made within six months after the date of publication in the designated patent office, which indicates that the international application has validly entered the national phase or such other date as specified in the Rules.[10] As each designated patent office has a different method of publishing such information the Registrar specified in the *Patent Rules*[11] the relevant date for these purposes. The actual date of valid entry is usually determined internally in each designated patent office and thus would not be a satisfactory date for this purpose.

Thus the date specified in the *Patents Rules* for the purposes of the European Patent Office and the United Kingdom Patent Office is the date of publication in their relevant official publications (European Patent Office Bulletin and the United Kingdom Patent Office Official Journal (Patents)) of data showing that an international application has entered the national phase.

The date specified in the *Patents Rules* for the purposes of the Chinese Patent Office is one of two dates. Where the international application is published by the World Intellectual Property Organisation in a language other than Chinese then the date is the date of publication by the Chinese Patent Office in its Patent Gazette of data showing that the international application has entered the national phase. If, however, the international application is published by the World Intellectual Property Organisation in Chinese then the other date is any date within six months after the date of issue by the Chinese Patent Office of the National Application Notification.[12] The position with regard to this alternative date is not too clear. In theory it seems that the alternate date may not be fixed but may be any date starting from the date of issue of the notification and ending on a date six months later.[13] If this interpretation is correct then an applicant can make an application at any time within six months of any date falling within six months of the date of issue of the National Application Notification. It seems unlikely that this was the intention and it will be safer for applicants to assume that application must be made within six months of the date of issue of the Notification.

Apart from the provisions outlined above and some modification of the documents to be filed, an international application is dealt with in the same way as a domestic application made to the designated patent office.

Right to apply for a standard patent

The new law differentiates between persons who may apply for the patent and those who may in fact be entitled to obtain the patent in Hong Kong. As this is a registration system, the new law, whilst recognising that different persons may have different rights to the patent in the two jurisdictions, requires a link between the applicant in the designated patent office and the applicant in Hong Kong.

Thus, the person who may apply for a standard patent is primarily the applicant for the patent in the designated patent office or his successor in title or any person who may be entitled to the patent in Hong Kong in preference to the designated patent office applicant. Any person may before the standard patent is granted apply to the court or the Registrar to determine any questions as to who may apply.[14]

Provisions as to applications for a standard and short-term patent generally

The standard and short-term patent applications can be withdrawn and the particulars amended in the manner specified before grant or before preparations for such grant are completed, subject to certain limitations.[15]

Maintenance of application for a standard patent

In order to remain pending, a published application for a standard patent must be maintained on a date falling five years after the date of publication and thereafter annually, on payment of a maintenance fee, provided the corresponding designated patent application is still pending. There are provisions for restoration of rights in the event of failure to pay the maintenance fee.

The first date on which the application must be maintained occurs on the first anniversary of the date of filing in the designated patent office falling five years after the date of publication of the application for the standard patent and thereafter annually.

An application cannot be maintained in the following cases:

- The corresponding designated patent application has been withdrawn or abandoned;
- There has been a final refusal to grant the patent by the designated patent office; or
- The corresponding designated patent has been granted by the designated patent office, unless the time for filing a request for a grant at the second stage in Hong Kong has not expired.[16]

Application for a short-term patent

Application is made to the Hong Kong Patents Registry by filing a request for the grant of a short-term patent supported, *inter alia*, by

- a specification including a description, one or more claims, but not exceeding one independent claim and four subsidiary claims and drawings, if any;
- an abstract; and
- a search report.

The search report as to the prior art must be made by a searching authority to be prescribed by the Registrar by regulation. The searching authorities currently appointed are the PCT international searching authorities and the designated patent offices.[17]

A filing date will be accorded after compliance with the minimum requirements. On compliance with the formalities the short-term patent will be granted. Applicants may, on filing, request a deferral of the grant of up to twelve (12) months.[18]

The Registrar is required only to ensure that the formal requirements of the application procedure are complied with.[19] The formality procedures mirror those that apply on an application for a standard patent. Thus the Hong Kong Patents Registry will first examine whether the minimum requirements are complied with and if so accord a filing date. Once the filing date is given the Registry will carry out an examination as to the formal requirements. The time periods will be the same and the provisions for further processing and restitution of rights in certain circumstances will apply.[20]

Application for a short-term patent based on an international application

Application for a short-term patent can also be made based on an international application under the PCT designating China. Application to the Hong Kong Patents Registry must be made within six months after the entry into the national phase in the Chinese Patent Office of the international application or such other date as prescribed by the Rules.[21] The other date has been prescribed by the Patents Rules as any date within six months after the date of issue of the National Application Notification by the Chinese Patent Office. Again it seems this date is not too clear. In theory it seems that the alternate date may not be fixed but may be any date starting from the date of issue of the notification and ending on a date six months later.[22] If this interpretation is correct then an applicant can make an application at any time within six months of any date falling within six months of the date of issue of the National Application Notification. It seems unlikely that this was the intention and it will be safer for applicants to assume that application must be made within six months of the date of issue of the Notification.

Application is made by filing a request for the grant of a short-term patent supported by

- a photocopy of the international application as published under the provisions of the PCT;
- a photocopy of the international search report as published under the provisions of the PCT;
- information on the date of entry of the international application into the national phase;
- a photocopy of the translation of the international application published by the Chinese Patent Office; and
- a photocopy of any information published by the Chinese Patent Office in respect of the international application.

The filing requirements under an international application are similar but the international application and search report will be accepted as the basis for the grant. The date of filing accorded the international application under the PCT will be the date of filing for the short-term patent for the purposes of the *Patents Ordinance*.

The procedures for processing and grant of a short-term patent presumably apply to an application for a short-term patent based on an international application. There appear to be some anomalies. For example, the Registrar is required to accord a filing date if the minimum requirements are complied with. In theory the Registrar could be required to accord a filing date even if the application was made more than six months after the date of entry into the national phase in the Chinese Patent Office of the international application. The Registrar would on examining the application then presumably be entitled to refuse to grant the short-term patent if it was not filed in due time even though this is not one of the formal requirements referred to in s 115 of the *Patents Ordinance*.

The actual date of entry into the national phase is not a matter of public record until details are published and this date may be difficult for practitioners and potential users of the invention to establish. As already indicated the date specified in the *Patents Rules* may not be clear but it is presumably intended that application should be made within six months after the date of issue by the Chinese Patent Office of the National Application Notification. It is not known when the issue of this Notification becomes a matter of public record.

Right to apply for a short-term patent

Any person may apply for a short-term patent.

Term of a standard patent

The standard patent is granted for a term of 20 years from the deemed date of filing, ie the date of filing of the corresponding application in the designated patent office, subject to renewal.[23]

Deemed date of filing a standard patent

After the standard patent is granted the new law defines the deemed date of filing of the standard patent application as the date of filing of the corresponding designated patent application in the designated patent office.[24] This is to be contrasted with the date of filing in Hong Kong of the request to record and request to register and grant.

Renewal of a standard patent

The standard patent to remain in force must be renewed three to four years after grant and thereafter annually, on payment of a renewal fee.

The first renewal is required on the first anniversary of the deemed date of filing, ie the date of filing of the corresponding designated patent application falling after the end of the third year after the grant of the standard patent. Thereafter renewal is required annually on the anniversary of the deemed date of filing.

The new law contains provisions for the payment of the renewal fee during the six months grace period and for restoration of standard patents that have lapsed due to failure to pay the renewal fee.[25]

Term of a short-term patent

The short-term patent is granted for a term of eight years from the date of filing the application, subject to renewal.[26]

Renewal of a short-term patent

To remain in force, the short-term patent must be renewed on payment of a renewal fee for the remaining four years of the term after the expiry of the fourth year from the date of filing the application for the short-term patent. The new law contains provisions for the payment of the renewal fee during the six months grace period and for restoration of short-term patents that have lapsed due to failure to pay the renewal fee.[27]

Rights given on grant of a patent

The proprietor of either a standard patent or a short-term patent has the right to prevent third parties from doing certain specified acts without his consent.

In essence the proprietor has the right to prevent others, without his consent, from making, putting on the market, using or importing a product which is the subject of a patent or from stocking that product whether to put this on the market in Hong Kong or elsewhere or otherwise. If the product is obtained directly by a process which is the subject of a patent then the same rights are given in relation to that product. If the subject matter of the patent is a process then the proprietor has the right to prevent others from using the process or offering the process for use in Hong Kong without his consent where it is known or obvious that such use of the process is not permitted without the consent of the proprietor. There are limitations on the rights given to the proprietor. Thus, for example, the proprietor does not have the right to prevent such use in relation to acts done privately for non-commercial purposes and acts done for experimental purposes relating to the subject matter of the patent.

The proprietor of a patent also has the right to prevent others from supplying in Hong Kong without his consent, the means for putting into effect the invention, where this relates to an essential element of the invention. This provision only applies in the case where it is obvious in the circumstances to a reasonable person that such means are suitable and can be used for the purpose of putting the invention into effect in Hong Kong. This provision does not apply in relation to a person who is entitled to work the invention in Hong Kong.[28]

These rights reflect the provisions of s 60 of the *Patents Act* 1977 and there is in essence no change between the rights given under the old law and the rights given under the new law.

Rights given on publication of an application for a standard patent

An applicant for a standard patent has, after publication and until grant, the same right to bring an action for infringement and to request damages as if the patent had been granted on the date of publication. However, no action can be brought until the patent has been granted.[29]

Remedies on infringement of a patent

The proprietor of either a standard or short-term patent has the right to bring an action for infringement. With any such an action, the usual common law remedies as codified in the *Patents Ordinance* are available. Such remedies include the right to request an injunction, an order for delivery up and damages. These remedies were all available under the old law under the common law but have now been codified in the new law.

Additional provisions for court proceedings in respect of a short-term patent

In addition to the above remedies, the new law contains some special provisions in respect of any court proceedings involving a short-term patent.[30]

In any such court proceedings the proprietor of the short-term patent is required to establish *prima facie* the validity of the short-term patent. The fact that the short-term patent has been granted will be of no account, but evidence that is sufficient to establish *prima facie* proof will, in the absence of evidence to the contrary, be sufficient. In addition, if in any such court proceedings an order is made in relation to interlocutory proceedings, either party may apply to the court to request a speedy trial.

Amendment of the specification of the standard and short-term patent

Application to amend the specification of a patent after grant (whether a standard or short-term patent) can be made to the court. The court may order such amendment subject to any conditions. If the amendment is granted then particulars must be filed with the Hong Kong Patents Registry.[31]

No amendment of the specification may include added matter and thus extend the subject of the application of the patent as filed and any such amendment will be invalid to the extent that it does contain added matter.[32]

Alternative procedure for amendment of standard patent

If the corresponding patent granted by the designated patent office is amended in prescribed opposition or revocation proceedings the proprietor is required to notify the Registrar within three months of such amendment.[33] If this is so filed, the Registrar is required to record this and advertise notice in the Gazette.

This is an alternative procedure to making an application to the court. If the application is made in the time period set the Registrar will record the amendment. If the proprietor fails to apply in the time period then application can still be made to the court. The court may however, take into account the failure to file under these provisions in considering whether to grant the application.

The prescribed opposition or rectification proceedings refer only to immediate post-grant proceedings.[34] They do not refer to other types of rectification procedure in the designated patent offices. Thus, this refers to opposition proceedings under Part V of the European Patent Convention and post-grant revocation proceedings to be made within six months of the grant under the Chinese Patent Law, namely Articles 41-44 of the Patent Law of the People's Republic of China and Rules 55 to 63 of the Implementing Regulations of the Patent Law.[35] There are no provisions for opposition in the United Kingdom Patent Office and consequently, these provisions will not apply to United Kingdom patents. The purpose of this provision is to provide a quicker and less expensive procedure to record amendments when these result from immediate post-grant procedures. This is based on the concept that the proceedings are considered to be part of the grant procedure. Thus ss 41 and 91(1)(i) of the *Patents Ordinance* are the only provisions which link the standard patent with the designated patent after grant.

No amendment of the specification under this alternate procedure may include added matter and thus extend the subject of the application of the patent as filed and any such amendment will be invalid to the extent that it does contain added matter.[36]

Amendment of the specification of the standard patent application

The claims, description and drawings of the application for a standard patent can be amended after the publication of the application for the standard patent and before grant or before preparations for grant are complete, but only in specified circumstances.

In particular application for amendment can only be made if the amendment is the same as an amendment made to the corresponding designated patent application by the designated patent office.[37]

No amendment of the specification may include added matter and thus extend the subject matter of the application of the patent as filed. Any such amendment will be invalid to the extent that it does contain added matter.[38]

Amendment of the specification of the short-term patent application

The applicant for a short-term patent may, before grant or before final preparations have been made for grant, of his own volition, amend the application upon making application to the Registrar. The Registrar will record this and on grant will also publish the specification and the application as filed.[39]

No amendment of the specification may include added matter and thus extend the subject of the application of the patent as filed and any such amendment will be invalid to the extent that it does contain added matter.[40]

Patentability of a patent

An invention is patentable as either a standard or short-term patent if it is new, involves an inventive step and is industrially applicable. Certain subject matter shall not be regarded as inventions and an invention that is contrary to *ordre public* will not be patentable. These provisions follow closely the similar provisions in the European Patent Convention. This reflects the current law and also the laws in this respect of the proposed designated patent offices.[41]

Novelty

An invention is new if it does not form part of the state-of-the-art. The state-of-the-art shall be taken to include everything made available to the public, whether in Hong Kong or elsewhere, whether orally or in writing, before the deemed date of filing of the standard or short-term patent application or, in either case if priority is claimed, before the date of priority.[42]

In addition, the *state-of-the-art* will comprise the subject matter of unpublished patent applications as filed in each of the designated patent offices and short-term patent applications as filed with the Registrar. A *whole contents approach* will be used to determine subject matter. For purposes of considering the novelty of an invention contained in a later patent application, the subject matter of an earlier application will be considered as part of the *state-of-the-art* as at the date of filing the later application in the relevant patent office, or at the date of priority, provided the earlier application filed before the date of filing of the later application and is published, as filed, in the relevant patent office after the date of filing or deemed date of filing.[43]

The effect of these provisions on a short-term patent based on an international application is not entirely clear. The date of filing such an application is deemed to be the international filing date given under the PCT. The definition of publication of the short-term patent is publication under s 118 unless the context requires otherwise.[44] A short-term patent based on an international application will have been published under the provisions of the PCT or in the Chinese Patent Office before it is filed in the Hong Kong Patents Registry. In view of this it seems clear that the subject matter of the invention will be considered as part of the state of the art as at the actual date of filing in Hong Kong under s 94(2) of the *Patents Ordinance*, but not as at the deemed date of filing under s 125(5). It seems the provisions of s 125(5) will save the short-term patent based on an international application from being liable to revocation for lack of novelty. Furthermore, it seems that the provisions of s 94(3)(c) also apply on the basis that the date of filing for the purposes of this section will be the deemed date of filing under s 125(5).

Non-prejudicial disclosure for the purpose of a patent

The new law contains provisions dealing with disclosures, which are to be considered as non-prejudicial for the purposes of assessing novelty.

Disclosures made no earlier than six months before the deemed date of filing of a standard patent application or the date of filing of a short-term patent application, which are not in good faith or arose as a result of being displayed at specified exhibitions, will not be taken into account for assessing novelty.

Different procedures apply for claiming such non-prejudicial disclosure for standard and short-term patents.[45]

Priority for patent applications

The new law contains provisions which give the short-term or standard patent applicant the right to claim a right of priority under the Paris

Convention on the basis of an earlier application filed in a Paris Convention country or in the country territory or area of a member of the World Trade Organisation.

The new law contains different provisions for claiming such right of priority for standard and short-term patent applications.

In the case of a standard patent, the applicant enjoys the same right of priority as he enjoys in the designated patent office provided the earlier application was filed in a Paris Convention country or in a World Trade Organisation member country[46], subject to claiming this right to priority when filing the request to record in Hong Kong.

A person who files an application for a short-term patent may enjoy a right of priority in respect of an earlier filing in a Paris Convention country or in a World Trade Organisation member country's territory or area for the twelve-month period after the date of filing the first application. Such a country must have been specified in the Schedule to the *Patents Ordinance*. Such priority must be claimed in accordance with the *Patent Rules* when filing the application.[47]

Right to a standard and short-term patent

The right to be granted a standard and short-term patent belongs to the inventor or his successor in title. This is to be contrasted with the right to apply referred to above.

The patent system is based on the first-to-file principle. Where two or more persons create an invention independently, the standard or short-term patent belongs to the person who filed first or, if priority is claimed, the earlier of the date of priority or filing date, in any of the designated patent offices or in the Hong Kong Patents Registry. In the case of an application for a standard patent this applies only if that application is published in Hong Kong.[48]

In the case of a short-term patent based on an international application the date of filing the short-term patent for these purposes will be the date of filing the international application and not the date of filing with the Hong Kong Patents Registry.

After the grant of a patent an application may be made to the court to decide the question of entitlement to the grant of a patent. Application can be made by any person who has the right to the patent or who claims such a right. The court may make such order as it thinks fit in the circumstances to give effect to its decision.

Revocation and putting validity in issue

A standard and short-term patent can be revoked and tested for validity on application to the court on the grounds specified.[49]

The main grounds for revocation of a patent are that

- the invention is not patentable;
- the patent was granted to a person not entitled;
- the subject matter of the patent extends beyond that disclosed in the application for the patent as filed;
- protection has been extended on an amendment; or
- the specification does not disclose the invention in a manner sufficiently clear and complete for it to be performed by a person skilled in the art.

As only a formality examination is carried out, two or more patents for the same invention could be granted. In certain cases, application for revocation may also be brought in the circumstances outlined where two or more standard patents or short-term patents for the same invention are so granted.

In addition to the above provisions, application for revocation can be made to the Registrar on the ground that the invention would be contrary to *ordre public* and thus not a patentable invention. The Registrar may determine the question or refer it to the court.[50]

Special provisions for revocation of a standard patent

If the corresponding designated patent has been revoked in the designated patent office in prescribed opposition or revocation proceedings the proprietor of a standard patent is required to file particulars of such revocation with the Registrar after publication of the revocation.[51] The Registrar will record notice of such filing and give notice of the fact of such filing in the Gazette. After such advertisement the standard patent will be revoked.

In addition any person, as an alternative to applying to the court, may apply to the Registrar for an order for revocation of the standard patent on the basis that the corresponding designated patent has been revoked by the designated patent office following such opposition or revocation proceedings. If the Registrar is satisfied that the designated patent has been so revoked he shall order revocation.[52] Before making such an order, the Registrar is required to give notice to the person registered as the proprietor of the patent and any other person the Registrar considers may have an interest in the patent. Any such person may oppose the revocation.[53]

The purpose of this provision is to give a quicker and less expensive alternative method of revocation where the patent is revoked on opposition or immediate post grant revocation provisions in the designated patent office. Sections 44 and 91(1)(i) of the *Patents Ordinance* are the only provisions with any link to the revocation of the parent patent after grant.

Revocation – summary

In summary, application for revocation is made to the court. However, application may alternatively be made to the Registrar

- if the grounds are that the invention is contrary to *ordre public*; or
- if the standard patent has been revoked in the designated patent office in prescribed opposition or revocation proceedings.

Putting validity in issue

The new law specifies the proceedings where validity may be put in issue.[54] These are stated to be

- As a defence in infringement proceedings;
- In proceedings for relief against groundless threats of infringement;
- Where a declaration as to non-infringement is claimed;
- In revocation proceedings; or
- In proceedings relating to government use.

Compulsory licensing of a standard patent

Any person may apply to the court for the grant of a compulsory licence of a standard patent on the grounds specified. Application can be made at any time after the expiration of three years after the grant of the standard patent.

The court may grant such a licence on the grounds specified if it is satisfied that

- an invention which can be worked on a commercial scale in Hong Kong is not being so worked,

- the proprietor of the patent will receive reasonable remuneration; and
- any person working or developing the invention in Hong Kong is not unfairly prejudiced.[55]

These provisions are in line with the requirements of the TRIPs Agreement as they relate to compulsory licensing.[56]

Working of an invention is in the main taken to include importing.[57]

Government use of a standard and short-term patent

If a period of extreme urgency is declared by the Chief Executive-in-Council, any person duly authorised by the Chief Executive may use the invention without the consent of the proprietor. The proprietor should be notified of such government use and receive reasonable remuneration. Any dispute with regard to such government use can be referred to the court.[58]

These provisions are in line with the requirements of the TRIPs Agreement as they relate to compulsory licensing

Nature of a patent and application for patents and transactions relating to them

A standard patent and a short-term patent and/or any application for such patent are considered to be personal property and can be dealt with as such. The patent or application for a patent can therefore be transferred, charged or licensed. Such transactions are to be recorded with the Hong Kong Patents Registry.

The *Patents Rules* set out the requirements for recording such transactions. The filing requirements, in line with those of the proposed Patent Law Treaty, provide that the Registrar will record these if the formality requirements are satisfied.

The new law introduces provisions setting out the effect of registration on priority in transactions and on infringement designed to encourage prompt filing of any such transactions.[59]

Language

An application for a standard and short-term patent can be made in either of the official languages, ie English or Chinese. The language of the application will then be the language of the proceedings before the Registrar.

The application in Hong Kong, in the case of an application for a standard patent does not have to be in the same official language as the language of the proceedings before the designated patent office.

The authentic text will be the text in the language of the proceedings before the Registrar. However, in the case of a standard patent, the authentic text of the standard patent will be the text of the designated patent in the language of the proceedings before the designated patent office. There are specific provisions dealing with the authentic text of a standard patent where the language of the proceedings before the designated patent office is not one of the official languages.

The new law allows for representation before the Hong Kong Patents Registry to be made in either language and for translations as appropriate in such circumstances. Certain data may on application for a patent or on recording transactions, be required in both languages to assist users of the system.[60] The details are set out in the *Patents Rules*.[61]

Register and search facilities

The Hong Kong Patents Registry is required to maintain a register of both standard patents and short-term patents giving details of the proprietor, the title of the invention and other relevant data. The register, the patent specification and the relevant file will be open to inspection subject to any restrictions which may be set out in the *Patents Rules* to ensure confidentiality in certain circumstances.[62]

Transitional provisions

The new law will contain provisions to deal with transitional arrangements. This is dealt with in Chapter 5.

Notes

1 Section 8 *Patents Ordinance.*

2 Section 15(6) *Patents Ordinance.*

3 Section 10 to 20 *Patents Ordinance.*

4 Sections 3 and 5 *Patents Ordinance.*

5 Sections 23 to 28 *Patents Ordinance.*

6 Section 11 *Patents Ordinance.*

7 Section 17 *Patents (General) Rules.*

8 Sections 28 to 30 *Patents Ordinance.*

9 Section 4(1) of *Patents Ordinance* (definition of designated patent application).

10 Section 16 *Patents Ordinance.*

11 Section 15 *Patents (General) Rules.*

12 Section 15(2(a)) *Patents (General) Rules.*

13 Section 15(2(a)) *Patents (General) Rules* and ss 15 and 16 *Patents Ordinance.*

14 Sections 12 to 14 *Patents Ordinance.*

15 Sections 31 to 32 and 121 to 122 *Patents Ordinance.*

16 Sections 33 to 35 *Patents Ordinance.*

17 Section 71 *Patents (General) Rules.*

18 Sections 113 to 119 *Patents Ordinance.*

19 Section 117 *Patents Ordinance.*

20 Section 123 *Patents Ordinance.*

21 Section 125 *Patents Ordinance.*

22 Sections 114 to 115 and 125 *Patents Ordinance.*

23 Section 39 *Patents Ordinance.*

24 Section 38 of the *Patents Ordinance* and s 2 of the *Patents Ordinance.*

25 Sections 39 to 41 *Patents Ordinance.*

26 Section 126 *Patents Ordinance.*

27 Sections 126 and 127 *Patents Ordinance.*

28 Sections 73 to 75 *Patents Ordinance.*

29 Section 88 *Patents Ordinance.*

30 Section 128 *Patents Ordinance.*

31 Section 46 *Patents Ordinance.*

32 Sections 102 to 103 *Patents Ordinance.*

33 Section 35 *Patents (General) Rules.*

34 Sections 36 and 54 *Patents (General) Rules.*

35 Sections 43 and 44 *Patents Ordinance.*

36 See note 32 above.

37 Section 31 *Patents Ordinance.*

38 See note 32 above.

39 Sections 120 and 122 *Patents Ordinance.*

40 See note 32 above.

41 Section 93 *Patents Ordinance.*

42 Section 94 *Patents Ordinance.*

43 Section 94(2) *Patents Ordinance.*

44 Section 5 *Patents Ordinance.*

45 Sections 95 and 109 *Patents Ordinance.*

46 Sections 98 to 99 *Patents Ordinance.*

47 Sections 110 and 111 *Patents Ordinance.*

48 Section 100 *Patents Ordinance.*

49 Sections 91 to 92 *Patents Ordinance.*

50 Section 49 *Patents Ordinance.*

51 Section 37 *Patents (General) Rules.*

52 Section 44 *Patents Ordinance.*

53 Section 37 *Patents (General) Rules.*

54 Section 101 *Patents Ordinance.*

55 Sections 64 to 67 *Patents Ordinance.*

56 Article 31 TRIPs Agreement.

57 Section 6(4) *Patents Ordinance* c/f s 64(2(c) of *Patents Ordinance* which refers to 'working by manufacture'.

58 Sections 68 to 72 *Patents Ordinance.*

59 Sections 50 to 52 and 87 *Patents Ordinance.*

60 Sections104 to 106 *Patents Ordinance.*

61 Section 56 *Patents (General) Rules.*

62 Sections 51 and 147 *Patents Ordinance* and ss 88 to 92 *Patents (General) Rules.*

5 Transitional Provisions

The underlying philosophy behind the transitional provisions is to ensure that the rights of proprietors or applicants for a patent granted or made before the commencement date, which could have been protected under the old law, are not prejudiced or lost under the new law.

The new law is prospective in effect. The *Patents Ordinance* specifically prohibits patent applications being the basis for a patent in Hong Kong published by a patent office before the date on which such office was designated.[1] Thus only proprietors of patent applications published by a designated patent office after the date it is designated can apply for a patent in Hong Kong.

Transitional provisions are, therefore, required. Firstly, to ensure the continued protection of patents registered under the old law. Secondly, to allow for the grant of a standard patent under the new law in respect of patents or patent applications made for a United Kingdom patent or a European patent (UK) which could not be registered under the new law but which would have been capable of being registered under the current law and thus protected in Hong Kong. Thirdly, to specify those provisions of the new law which are to apply to deemed standard patents or standard patents granted under the transitional provisions.

The transitional arrangements under the new law accordingly provide for all existing registered patents that are in force in the United Kingdom on the commencement date to be deemed standard patents. There will be an automatic transfer of these patents to the new register by the Hong Kong Patents Registry. Deemed standard patents will no longer be dependent on the United Kingdom law and the relevant provisions of the new law will apply.

In addition, the transitional provisions under the new law allow an applicant to apply for the grant of a standard patent based on

- the registration of a United Kingdom patent or a European patent (UK) granted prior to the commencement date which is entitled to be protected under the old law; or
- a patent granted after the commencement date pursuant to an application made and published prior to that date for a United Kingdom patent or a European patent (UK), which, if granted before the commencement date, could have been protected under the old law.

The transitional provisions will apply, suitably modified, to standard patents granted under the transitional provisions.

Application for a standard patent under the provisions of the new law[2] can be made in respect of all applications published by a designated patent office after designation by the Chief Executive-in-Council or the commencement date, whichever is the later. Thus, under the new law, the trigger date is date of publication rather than date of application.

The designated patent offices are the Chinese Patent Office, the European Patent Office for patents designating the United Kingdom and the United Kingdom Patent Office. Applications published by these offices after the commencement date can be used as the basis for granting a patent under the new law, whether the application was made before or after that date.

For this reason, it was necessary to provide transitional provisions to deal with applications made and published before the commencement date by the United Kingdom Patent Office or the European Patent Office, but not for unpublished applications made prior to that date.

In summary, the new law introduces new provisions for the grant of patents in Hong Kong. On commencement, proprietors of patents registered under the old law or of patents or patent applications that could have been registered under the old law will have to assess what action needs to be taken under the new law to ensure appropriate patent protection for their inventions in Hong Kong. If the application is made and published before 27 June 1997 the proprietor must apply under the transitional provisions. If the application is published after 27 June 1997 then the proprietor must apply under the new law. The relevant provisions of the new law will apply, as modified, to standard patents granted under the transitional provisions.

Outline of Transitional Provisions

The transitional provisions of the new law deal with the following points:

- The repeal of the *Registration of Patents Ordinance*;
- The continued application of the old law in respect of acts done before the commencement of the new law in relation to patents registered under the old law;
- The continued protection of patents registered and in force in the United Kingdom on the commencement date under the old law;
- The deemed grant of a standard patent in respect of existing registered patents;
- The grant of a standard patent based on:
  - (i) patents granted prior to the commencement date which are entitled to protection under the old law;
  - (ii) patents granted after the commencement date pursuant to an application made and published prior to that date, which, if granted before the commencement date, could have been protected under the old law; or
  - (iii) patents granted after the commencement date pursuant to an application made under the United Kingdom *Patents Act* 1949; and
- The application of the new law and the continued application of the old law as appropriate to patents registered under the old law and standard patents granted under the transitional provisions.

Patents Ordinance

The *Patents Ordinance* provides for

- the repeal of the *Registration of Patents Ordinance*;
- certain transitional provisions related to government use and infringement including the continued application of the old law in respect of acts done before the commencement date; and

- the Chief Executive-in-Council to have the power to make Rules to be approved by the Legislative Council governing a number of aspects relating to the transitional provisions.

The Rules made by the Governor-in-Council, known as the *Patents (Transitional Arrangements) Rules*,[3] contain detailed provisions for

- patents registered under the old law and in force on the commencement date (existing registered patents) to be a deemed standard patent;
- the grant of a standard patent in certain circumstances under the transitional provisions; and
- the application of the *Patents Ordinance* and the continued application of the *Registration of Patents Ordinance* to certain types of standard patents granted or deemed to be granted under the transitional provisions.

Reference in this Chapter to the *transitional provisions* includes reference to the transitional arrangements provided for under the *Patents Ordinance* and the *Patents (Transitional Arrangements) Rules* (Transitional Rules) and reference to 'the commencement date' is a reference to the commencement date and coming into operation of the *Patents Ordinance*, namely 27 June 1997.[4]

United Kingdom Patents Act 1949 and Patents Act 1977

The *Registration of Patents Ordinance* provides for the registration of patents granted under the *Patents Act* 1949 (1949 Act) or under the *Patents Act* 1977 (1977 Act) including European patents (UK) treated as granted under s 77 of the 1977 Act.[5]

The 1977 Act was enacted on 29 July 1977 and came into force on 1 June 1978. The 1977 Act repealed the 1949 Act but preserved certain of its provisions both in respect of patents applied for and granted under the 1949 Act and applications applied for under the 1949 Act and granted under the 1977 Act pursuant to that application.

Thus the old law provided for the registration of patents granted under the 1977 Act pursuant to an application under that Act and for European patents (UK) which took effect under that Act (1977 Act patents) and for patents granted under the 1949 Act or the 1977 Act pursuant to an application made under the 1949 Act (1949 Act patents).

It is anticipated that some of these 1949 Act patents are registered in Hong Kong and could still be in force until 31 May 1998. It is, in theory, also possible that there are still pending applications under the 1949 Act which have not yet been granted by the United Kingdom Patent Office but which could still mature to grant.

The 1977 Act preserved certain provisions of the 1949 Act for the purposes of patents granted and patent applications under the 1949 Act which were in force or still pending on the day the act came into effect. Some of these preserved provisions are spent but some still remain in force. The remaining provisions relate to the complete specification, priority date of claims of the complete specification, the search for anticipation by prior claim and by previous publication and the examination of the application. These provisions primarily concern the patentability of 1949 Act patents.[6]

As outlined, there are differences between 1949 Act and 1977 Act patents. The transitional provisions of the new law caters for these differences to ensure that 1949 Act patents registered under the old law or used as the basis for the grant of a standard patent under the transitional provisions continue to be protected under the new law. If special provisions were not made such patents would become liable to revocation under the new law. Accordingly, some provisions of the new law do not apply to 1949 Act patents, which are deemed to be standard patents, or standard patents granted under the transitional provisions of the new law.

The transitional provisions give no right to the Hong Kong courts to revoke or amend standard patents based on a 1949 Act patent except under the revocation provisions in s 49 of the *Patents Ordinance,* which allow for revocation on the grounds that an invention is contrary to *ordre public*. However, there are provisions that allow for standard patents based on a 1949 Act patent to be revoked or amended if it is revoked or amended in the United Kingdom.[7]

Patents Covered by the Transitional Provisions

There are various categories of patents or patent applications provided for in the transitional provisions of the *Patents Ordinance*. These categories have been further subdivided to deal with the differences between 1949 Act patents and 1977 Act patents. The transitional provisions therefore establish the method of protection for each category and specify which parts of the new law apply to each respective category.

Section 159 of the *Patents Ordinance* defines the various categories. Sections 3 to 9 of the *Patents (Transitional Arrangements) Rules* provide for different methods of obtaining protection for patents falling within these categories and for the application of the new law, suitably modified as set out in Schedules 1 to 5 of the *Patents (Transitional Arrangements) Rules* and ss 111 and 112 and Schedule 3 of the *Patents (General) Rules*.

These categories based on the definitions contained in s 159 the *Patents Ordinance* are listed below:

- *Existing registered patents* being 1949 or 1977 Act patents registered under the old law and in force on the commencement date;
- *Pending applications for registration under the repealed Ordinance* being applications made under the old law pending registration at the commencement date;
- *Existing 1949 or 1977 Act patents* being patents granted by the United Kingdom Patent Office prior to the commencement date, capable of being registered under the old law, but not , in fact, so registered;
- *Published applications for a 1977 Act patent* being published applications for 1977 Act patents pending in the United Kingdom Patent Office or the European Patent Office at the commencement date. The patents granted pursuant to these applications must have been eligible for registration under the *Registration of Patents Ordinance*. This term also covers patents granted pursuant to that application after the commencement date; and
- *Existing applications for a 1949 Act patent* being existing patent applications under the 1949 Act still pending before the United Kingdom Patent Office at the commencement date and patents granted pursuant to that application after the commencement date.

The following table sets out the relevant provisions of the *Patents (Transitional Arrangements) Rules*, which deal with the method of protection and application of the new law for the various categories.

Patents (Transitional Arrangements) Rules			**Patent (General) Rules**
Category of Patents	**Method of protection**	**Application of the new law and modifications**	**Application of the new law and modifications**
Existing registered 1949 Act patent	ss 3, 4, 13 and 14	Part I Schedule 1	
Existing registered 1977 Act patent	ss 3, 4, 13 and 14	Part II Schedule 1	
Pending application for Registration under the repealed Ordinance	s 5		
Existing 1949 Act patent	s 6	Parts 1 and II Schedule 2	s 111 and Schedule 3 Part I
Existing 1977 Act patent	s 6	Parts I and III Schedule 2	s 111 and Schedule 3 Part I
Published application for 1977 Act patent	ss 7 and 8	Parts I and II Schedule 3 and Parts I and II Schedule 4	ss 111 and 112 and Schedule 3 Part I and II
Existing application for a 1949 Act patent	s 9	Parts I and II Schedule 5	s 111 and Schedule 3 Part I

In this outline we will first deal separately with each category in establishing the method of protection and the term of each category of standard patent and then deal with the application of the main aspects of the new law to these categories.

Method of Protection

Existing 1949 Act and 1977 Act registered patents under the new law

Existing registered patents are patents granted by the United Kingdom Patent Office under the 1949 Act or the 1977 Act, including European patents (UK) which take effect under the 1977 Act

- which have been registered under the *Registration of Patents Ordinance* prior to the commencement date; and
- which are still in force in the United Kingdom on the commencement date or which, if not renewed in the United Kingdom, are capable of being renewed or restored to the register under the United Kingdom law.

Under the new law, every existing 1949 Act and 1977 Act registered patent will be deemed to be and treated as if it were a standard patent granted under the new law and its particulars will be deemed to be entered on the register.[8] The specification of the invention in an existing registered patent will be taken to be the specification as amended in the United Kingdom as at the commencement date, whether or not details of the amendment have been filed in the United Kingdom.[9]

On or after the commencement date the Registrar will automatically enter on the Register the particulars of every such existing registered patent deemed to be a standard patent. The Registrar will take all reasonable steps to ensure that all existing registered patents are entered on the register.[10] The specification of the patent will be taken as the specification as amended in the United Kingdom on or before the commencement date, whether or not details of the amendment have been filed in Hong Kong.[11] However, no amendment or revocation in the United Kingdom, which takes place after the commencement date will have effect in Hong Kong after that date.[12] This is subject to the special amendment or revocation provisions in Hong Kong for standard patents based on 1949 Act patents after amendment or revocation in the United Kingdom.

The new law contains provisions to enable the Registrar, either on his own initiative, or on application by any person, to delete from the register any details relating to a deemed standard patent on the grounds that it was not in fact an existing registered patent. No such deletion may take place without giving notice to the proprietor named in the register and giving him an opportunity to be heard.[13]

The Registrar may, on application by the proprietor of an existing registered patent, add the details deemed to be entered in the register on the grounds that the patent is in fact an existing registered patent and accordingly a deemed standard patent.[14] In the event of addition to the register, the proprietor's rights are not affected except that in certain circumstances the rights of third parties who have commenced use are protected.[15]

An existing registered patent will remain in force for a term of 20 years, subject to renewal, calculated in the case of

- a 1977 Act patent, from the date of filing the application in the United Kingdom Patent Office or the European Patent Office; and
- a 1949 Act patent, from the date of filing the complete specification under the 1949 Act.

The existing registered patent, in order to remain in force, will be subject to renewal on the anniversary of the date of filing the application or the complete specification falling after the expiry of the third year after the commencement date. Thus, first renewal will fall due after 27 June 2000. In effect standard patents based on 1949 Act patents will not be renewable.[16]

Summary

The provisions can be summarised as follows:

- An existing registered patent will, under the new law, be deemed a standard patent under the *Patents Ordinance* and will be independent of United Kingdom patent law;
- The Hong Kong Patents Registry will, in conjunction with the United Kingdom Patent Office, take all reasonable steps to enter the particulars of every standard patent on the register; and
- There is no difference in treatment between 1949 Act and 1977 Act patents, but the date from which the term of the deemed standard patent starts will differ.

In a major departure from the old law, an existing registered patent will be subject to renewal in Hong Kong in order to remain in force. The first renewal will fall due on the first anniversary of the filing date after the commencement date and thereafter annually. This means that first renewal will fall due after 27 June 2000 and that in practice standard patents based on a 1949 Act patent will not be renewable.

Section 106 of the *Patents (General) Rules* specifies the deemed standard patent particulars that must be entered in the register. It seems likely that, in the event of any conflict between the United Kingdom Patent Office records and the Hong Kong Patents Registry records, the proprietor particulars entered on the Hong Kong register maintained under the *Registration of Patents Ordinance* as at the commencement date will be the particulars entered on the register under the new law. This will be so even if such particulars differ from the particulars entered in the United Kingdom Patent Office Register, on the basis that ownership of the patent in Hong Kong may differ from that in the United Kingdom.

Action by owner of patent

The proprietor of an existing registered patent does not have to take any action on the introduction of the new law. It would, however, be advisable for such proprietor to check that the patent is in fact entered in the register and to ensure the accuracy of the particulars entered in the register. It will be of particular importance to check the particulars are on the register in Hong Kong if the existing registered patent is renewed during the six months grace period or restored to the register in the United Kingdom.

The deemed standard patent will have to be renewed under the new law. The renewal period will be annually after an initial three-year grace period, which expires on 27 June 2000.

Pending applications for registration under the repealed Ordinance

A *pending application for registration* is an application for registration under the *Registration of Patents Ordinance*, which has been applied for but not registered prior to the commencement date. Under the transitional provisions the application will continue to be processed under the old law. The patent, on registration, will be deemed to have been registered the day before the commencement date.[17]

On registration it will be considered an existing registered patent. The provisions outlined above in relation to an existing registered patent will apply. Thus, on registration, the particulars of the patent will automatically be entered in the new Register and it will be deemed a standard patent. No infringement action arises, however, in respect of an infringement that occurred before the issue date of the registration certificate.[18]

Action by owner of patent

Any person who has applied for registration of a patent under the old law, which has not been registered prior to the commencement date, must comply with the registration requirements of the old law. The patent will be considered an existing registered patent and a deemed standard patent once it is registered. The applicant is not required to take any action in this respect.

No infringement action can be commenced until the certificate is issued.

Existing 1949 or 1977 Act patents

Existing 1949 or 1977 Act patents are patents

- that have been granted, prior to the commencement date, by the United Kingdom Patent Office under the 1949 Act or 1977 Act (including European patents (UK) which take effect under the 1977 Act;
- which were capable of being registered under the *Registration of Patents Ordinance* at the commencement date; but
- for which no such application for registration has been made before the commencement date.[19]

Only those patents which could be registered under the *Registration of Patents Ordinance* at the commencement date, namely 27 June 1997, but which have not been so registered are included in the definition of existing 1949 Act and 1977 Act patents. Patents granted more than five years before the commencement date will not fall within this category.

The transitional provisions of the new law provide that a standard patent can be granted based on the registration of the existing 1949 or 1977 Act patent.[20]

The grantee of an existing 1949 or 1977 Act patent or any person deriving his right from such grantee by assignment, transmission or other operation of law may, under the transitional provisions, make an application for a standard patent by requesting the Registrar to register that patent and grant a standard patent. Any such request must be made within 12 months after the commencement date, namely by 12 June 1998, or within five years after the date of grant of the existing patent, whichever is the earlier.[21]

The effect is that application for a standard patent based on an existing patent must be made within 12 months after the commencement date, namely before 27 June 1998, but in any event not more than five years after the grant of the existing 1949 or 1977 Act patent.

The application is made by requesting the registration of the existing patent and grant of a standard patent under the provisions, as modified of the *Patents Ordinance*, for making an application for a standard patent at the second stage. Thus the modified application procedures[22] will, in the main, follow the application procedures under the new law, but for the purposes of this category of transitional patent, only the second stage procedures are required.

The application must be made by the grantee of the existing 1949 or 1977 Act patent or any person deriving his right from such grantee by assignment, transmission or other operation of law. This follows the language used in the *Registration of Patents Ordinance* to describe the person entitled to apply for registration under the old law.

On compliance with the formality requirements a standard patent will be granted for a term of 20 years,[23] subject to renewal, calculated in the case of

- a 1977 Act patent from the date of filing of the application in the United Kingdom Patent Office or the European Patent Office; and
- a 1949 Act patent from the date of filing the complete specification under the 1949 Act.

Summary

In summary, an existing 1949 or 1977 Act patent is one granted by the United Kingdom Patent Office under either the 1949 Act or the 1977 Act not more than five years before the commencement date and which could be, but has not been, registered under the old law.

Under the transitional provisions of the new law a standard patent can be granted based on the registration of an existing 1949 or 1977 Act patent. Application must be made within the specified period after the commencement date or within five years of the grant, whichever is earlier. Thus under the new law a proprietor who has not registered under the old law can apply for the grant of a standard patent under the new law within 12 months of the commencement date, namely before 27 June 1998, but no later than 5 years after grant. The new law's procedures will apply, subject to modification.

Action by owner of patent
The proprietor of a patent granted by the United Kingdom Patent Office before the commencement date could opt to apply for protection of his invention under the old law before the commencement date or under the new law after that date. If application was not made under the old law prior to the commencement date, application must be made under the new law.

The application procedures and fees are similar under the new law, although filing under the transitional provisions will mean that first renewal may fall slightly later. There are no particular advantages or disadvantages in filing before or after the commencement date.

The major effect of the new law on existing patents is that the time period for making an application to protect a patent under the old law may be curtailed. Under the old law the time period was five years from the date of grant. Under the new law the time period is within 12 months after 27 June 1997, but in any event not more than five years after grant. As a result, proprietors of patents granted up to three years before the commencement date will have to make a decision before 27 June 1998 as to whether to protect their patent in Hong Kong. This is earlier than was formerly required.

Published application for a 1977 Act patent

A published application for a 1977 Act patent is an application for a patent made to the United Kingdom Patent Office or to the European Patent Office designating the United Kingdom

- which has been published prior to the commencement date; and
- in respect of which a patent under the 1977 Act (including European patents (UK) which take effect under the Patents Act 1977) could be granted.

Under the transitional provisions of the new law a standard patent can be granted based on the registration of the patent granted pursuant to a published application for a 1977 Act patent.[24]

The person named as an applicant in the published application or any person deriving his right from such grantee by assignment, transmission or other operation of law may make an application for grant of a standard patent under the transitional provisions of the new law. There are two alternative procedures for filing. In either case application must be made within the specified periods of time after the commencement date.[25]

Under the normal procedures covered by s 7 of the *Patents (Transitional Arrangements) Rules*, application must be made within 18 months of the commencement date. Under the alternative procedures covered by s 8 of the *Patents (Transitional Arrangements) Rules* application must be made within six months of the grant of a patent that was granted by the United Kingdom Patent Office within 12 months after the commencement date.

Using the normal procedures, an application for a standard patent based on a published application for a 1977 Act patent must be made within 18 months after the commencement date, under the provisions of the *Patents Ordinance*, as modified by the Transitional Rules.[26]

At the first stage, application in Hong Kong is made by requesting the Registrar to enter a record of that application in the register within 18 months of the commencement date, namely before 27 December 1998. Application is made at the second stage within six months after grant of the corresponding patent by requesting the Registrar to register that patent and to grant a standard patent.[27]

The application must be made by the person named as the applicant in the published application for a 1977 Act patent or any person deriving his right from such applicant by assignment, transmission or other operation of law.

An alternative application procedure is provided in respect of a published application for a 1977 Act patent. This alternative procedure applies where the 1977 Act patent is granted pursuant to that published application within 12 months after the commencement date.[28]

If the patent is granted pursuant to a published application by the United Kingdom Patent Office or by the European Patent Office in respect of a European patent (UK) within 12 months after the commencement date, then application may be made for a standard patent within six months of the grant of that 1977 Act patent.[29]

Application is made by requesting the Registrar to register that 1977 Act patent and grant a standard patent. The *Patents Ordinance* second stage application procedures will apply, as modified by the Transitional Rules.[30]

The application must be made by the grantee of the patent or any person deriving his right from such grantee by assignment, transmission or other operation of law.

On compliance with the formality requirements a standard patent based on a published application for a 1977 Act patent will be granted for a term of 20 years, subject to renewal, from the date of filing of the application in the United Kingdom Patent Office or the European Patent Office.

Summary

In summary, a published application for a 1977 Act patent is an application which has been made for a patent under the 1977 Act and which has been published before the commencement date, namely 27 June 1997, by the United Kingdom Patent Office or the European Patent Office, respectively.

Under the transitional provisions of the new law a standard patent can be granted based on the registration of the patent granted, pursuant to that published application. An applicant may use either the normal or alternative procedures.

Application is made by the person named as applicant in the published application to the Hong Kong Patents Registry under the provisions of the *Patents Ordinance* as amended by the Transitional Rules. On compliance with the formality requirements the standard patent will be granted.

Action by owner of patent

The proprietor of a published application for a 1977 Act patent, if the invention is to be protected in Hong Kong, must file an application for a standard patent within 18 months after the commencement date, namely before 27 December 1998. If such application is not made within that period then a patent cannot be obtained in Hong Kong.

Alternatively, if a patent is granted before 27 June 1998 (within 12 months after the commencement date), pursuant to a published 1977 Act patent application, then instead of following the two stage procedure the proprietor can file, within six months of the date of grant of the 1977 Act patent, under the second stage procedure only. This is obviously a simpler and more cost effective procedure where the patent is to be granted before 27 June 1998.

The time period for making an application where the application is filed but not granted before the commencement date is substantially curtailed. Under the old law, application was made after grant. Under the new law, application is to be made after publication. If the application is published before the commencement date, then the application must be filed in the specified period after the commencement date.

Under the old law the owner of an invention needed to take action to protect the invention only after the patent was granted in the United Kingdom. The application procedures under the new law are different. Under the new law an applicant is required to file the application within six months after the publication of the patent application in the designated patent office. The new law only applies, however, to applications published by the designated patent office after the designated patent office has been designated under the *Patents Ordinance*.

The provisions relating to applications published before the commencement date are required to ensure that owners of inventions who have taken steps to protect their inventions by applying for a patent to the United Kingdom Patent Office or the European Patent Office designating the United Kingdom can obtain a standard patent under the new law and do not lose their rights in this respect.

Existing application for a 1949 Act patent

An *existing application for a 1949 Act patent* refers to an application for a patent made to the United Kingdom Patent Office under the 1949 Act which is still pending at the commencement date and for which a patent has not been granted by the United Kingdom Patent Office. Under the transitional provisions of the new law a standard patent can be granted based on the registration of the patent, granted by the United Kingdom Patent Office after the commencement date, pursuant to the existing application for a 1949 Act patent.

If, after the commencement date, the patent is granted, then the grantee of the resulting 1949 Act patent or any person deriving his right from such grantee by assignment, transmission or other operation of law may, under the transitional provisions, make an application for a standard patent by requesting the Registrar to register that patent and grant a standard patent.[31]

Any such request must be made within six months after the grant of the patent[32] but in any event not later than 20 years from the date of filing the complete specification under the 1949 Act.

An application for a standard patent based on the existing application for a 1949 Act patent must be made within the specified period after the date of the grant of the 1949 Act patent by the United Kingdom Patent Office. An application cannot be made more than 20 years after the filing of the complete specification under the 1949 Act and the 1977 Act.

The application is made by requesting the registration of the patent granted pursuant to the existing application for a 1949 Act patent and for grant of a standard patent under the provisions, as modified, of the *Patents Ordinance* for making an application at the second stage.[33]

The application must be made by the grantee of the 1949 Act patent or any person deriving his right from such grantee by assignment, transmission or other operation of law.

On compliance with the formality requirements a standard patent will be granted for a term of 20 years from the date of filing the complete specification under the 1949 Act. There will be no renewal.

Summary

In summary, an existing application for a 1949 Act patent is an application for a patent under the 1949 Act which has not been granted by the United Kingdom Patent Office at the commencement date. Under the transitional provisions a standard patent can be granted based on the registration of the patent granted by the United Kingdom Patent Office after 27 June 1997, pursuant to that application.

Application for registration of that patent and the grant of a standard patent must be made within six months, after the grant of the patent, but not later than 20 years from the date of filing the complete specification pursuant to the 1949 Act.

Action by owner of patent

The proprietor of a patent granted by the United Kingdom Patent Office after 27 June 1997 pursuant to an application made under the 1949 Act can apply for the registration of that patent and grant of a standard patent.

Such application cannot be made after the term of the patent would have in any event have expired. The term of all 1949 Act patents will expire by 31 May 1998.

As mentioned above, 1949 Act patents may be granted even after the commencement date. The proprietors of such patents would have been able to obtain a patent under the old law and consequently should be able to obtain a standard patent under the new law.

Application of the New Law and Continued Application of Old Law under the Transitional Provisions

The *Patents Ordinance* and the *Patents (Transitional Arrangements) Rules* provide for

- the continued application of the old law to certain acts done before the commencement date in relation to existing registered patents or pending applications for registration under the old law;
- the application of the new law to deemed standard patents and standard patents granted under the transitional provisions; and
- special provisions for deemed standard patents or standard patents granted under the transitional provisions based on 1949 Act patents.

The main aspects of the transitional provisions relating to the application of the new law to the different categories of transitional patents are outlined below.

Application procedures for a standard patent[34] (ss 15-27 Patents Ordinance)

The application procedures of the *Patents Ordinance* will apply to an application for a standard patent under the transitional provisions subject to suitable modifications.[35] The modifications will be designed to ensure that the procedures can apply to patents granted under the transitional provisions. None of the application procedures apply to an existing registered patent that is deemed to be a standard patent by operation of law.

The modifications cover a number of factors and are set out in detail in Schedules 1 to 5 of the *Patents (Transitional Arrangements) Rules.* A major modification is that the first stage procedures[36] will not apply to applications for a standard patent under the transitional provisions based on

- an existing 1949 or 1977 Act patent;
- a patent granted within 12 months after the commencement date pursuant to a published application for a 1977 Act patent using the alternative procedure; or
- a patent granted pursuant to an existing application for a 1949 Act patent.

Another important modification relates to the time periods for taking initial action. For example, application for a standard patent pursuant to a published 1977 Act application must be made within 18 months after the commencement date rather than six months after publication.[37] Other modifications are primarily for drafting purposes to ensure that the relevant sections of the *Patents Ordinance* do in fact apply, for example, by ensuring that reference to a designated patent office is a reference to the United Kingdom Patent Office.

Maintenance of an application for standard patent[38] (ss 33-35 Patents Ordinance).

The provisions in the *Patents Ordinance* relating to maintenance of an application will only apply to an application for a standard patent based on a published application for a 1977 Act patent that is filed under the normal procedures.[39] The requirement to maintain an application will not apply to any other type of application for a standard patent under the transitional provisions.

Right to apply for grant of a standard patent[40] (s 12 Patents Ordinance)

The right to apply for a standard patent, as opposed to the right to the patent, under the transitional provisions of the *Patents Ordinance* vests in the grantee or any person deriving his right from such grantee by assignment, transmission or other operation of law when application is based on

- an existing 1949 or 1977 Act patent;[41]
- a patent granted within the specified period after the commencement date pursuant to a published application for a 1977 Act patent using the alternative procedure;[42] or
- a patent granted pursuant to an existing application for a 1949 Act patent.[43]

The right to apply at the first stage, in the case of an application based on a published application for a 1977 Act patent using the normal procedures, vests in the person named in that published application or any person deriving his right from such applicant by assignment, transmission or other operation of law.[44]

The language follows the *Registration of Patents Ordinance* and differs to some extent from the provisions in the *Patents Ordinance*. In the main it seems unlikely that in practical terms there will be any substantial difference between the two.

Deemed date of filing[45] (s 38 Patents Ordinance)

The provisions of the *Patents Ordinance*, suitably modified, provide that the deemed date of filing of all transitional patents, ie existing registered patents deemed to be standard patents and standard patents granted under the transitional provisions, will be the date of filing of the complete specification of the corresponding 1949 Act patent or the date of filing the corresponding 1977 Act patent.[46]

Renewal of a standard patent[47] (s 39 Patents Ordinance)

Transitional standard patents, ie deemed standard patents and standard patents granted under the transitional provisions must, to remain in force, be renewed on payment of a renewal fee.

Existing registered patents that are deemed standard patents will have to be renewed. The first renewal is required on the first anniversary of the application filing date falling after 27 June 2000, being the expiry of the third year following the commencement date.[48]

The renewal provisions of the *Patents Ordinance*, subject to modification as necessary, will apply to standard patents granted under the transitional provisions. The first renewal is required on the first anniversary of the date of filing the application in the designated patent office falling after the end of the third year after the grant of the standard patent. Thereafter, renewal is required annually on the anniversary of the filing date.[49]

These renewal provisions will not apply to existing 1949 Act registered patents which are deemed standard patents or standard patents granted under the transitional provisions which are based on 1949 Act patents.[50]

Employees' inventions[51] (ss 57-61 Patents Ordinance)

The provisions relating to employees' inventions do not apply to any of the transitional standard patents.[52]

Rights and remedies given in respect of a standard patent[53] (ss 80-83 Patents Ordinance)

The rights given to the proprietor of a standard patent under the *Patents Ordinance* will apply to all transitional patents, ie existing registered patents which are deemed standard patents and standard patents granted under the transitional provisions.[54]

Acts of infringement in respect of an existing registered patent which occur before the commencement date will be determined in accordance with the old law.[55]

Rights and remedies given on publication of an application for a standard patent[56] (s 88 Patents Ordinance)

The rights and remedies given on publication under the *Patents Ordinance* will be given only to the applicant for a standard patent under the transitional provisions based on a published application for a 1977 Act patent where the normal procedure is used and the alternative procedure is not adopted.[57]

These provisions will not apply to

- existing 1949 Act or 1977 Act registered patents which are deemed standard patents;
- standard patents based on an existing 1949 or 1977 Act patent; or
- standard patents based on patents granted pursuant to an existing application for a 1949 Act patent.

Amendment of the specification of the standard patent*[58] *(s 46 Patents Ordinance)

The provisions for amending the specification of a standard patent after grant on application to the court apply to

- existing registered 1977 Act patents which are deemed standard patents;
- standard patents based on an existing 1977 Act patent; or
- standard patents based on patents granted pursuant to a published application for a 1977 Act patent.

These provisions do not apply

- to existing 1949 Act registered patents which are deemed standard patents;
- standard patents based on existing 1949 Act patents; or
- standard patents based on patents granted pursuant to an existing application for a 1949 Act patent.

Amendment following prescribed opposition proceedings*[59] *(s 43 Patents Ordinance)

These provisions will apply to

- standard patents based on existing 1977 Act patents; or
- a standard patent granted based on patents granted pursuant to a published application for a 1977 Act patent, whether under the normal or alternative procedures.

These provisions will not apply to

- existing registered 1949 Act or 1977 Act patents which are deemed to be standard patents;
- standard patents based on existing 1949 Act patents; or
- standard patents based on patents granted pursuant to an existing application for a 1949 Act patent.

However, these provisions, specifically modified,[60] will apply to standard patents based on 1949 Act patents. Thus, if the corresponding

1949 Act patent is amended in the United Kingdom pursuant to amendment or revocation proceedings in respect of the 1949 Act patent under the 1977 Act, then application can be made by any person to the Registrar for a revocation order or to file the amendment, on the grounds that such patent has been revoked or amended in the United Kingdom.

Amendment of standard patent application[61] *(s 31 Patents Ordinance)*

These provisions will apply[62] to:

- an application for a standard patent pursuant to a published application for a 1977 Act patent made under the normal procedures;
- standard patents based on existing 1949 or 1977 Act patents;
- standard patents based on patents granted pursuant to a published application for a 1977 Act patent using the alternative procedure; or
- standard patents based on patents granted pursuant to an existing application for a 1949 Act patent.

Although these provisions apply to all these types of standard patents, in practical terms they are only relevant to standard patent applications made pursuant to published 1977 Act patent applications.

These provisions do not apply to existing registered 1949 Act or 1977 Act patents that are deemed to be standard patents.

Patentability of a standard patent[63] *(ss 93-97 Patents Ordinance)*

These provisions, including the provisions relating to non-prejudicial disclosure and priority, apply to

- existing registered 1977 Act patents which are deemed standard patents;
- standard patents based on existing 1977 Act patents; and
- standard patents based on patents granted pursuant to published 1977 Act patent applications.

These provisions do not apply to

- existing 1949 Act registered patents that are deemed standard patents;
- standard patents based on existing 1949 Act patents; and
- standard patents based on patents granted pursuant to an existing application for a 1949 Act patent.

There are special provisions dealing with the priority as between 1949 Act and 1977 Act patents.[64]

Right to a standard and short-term patent[65] (s 100 Patents Ordinance)

These provisions apply to

- existing registered 1977 Act patents which are deemed standard patents;
- standard patents based on existing 1977 Act patents; and
- standard patents based on patents granted pursuant to a published application for a 1977 Act patent whether under the normal or alternative procedures.

These provisions do not apply to

- existing 1949 Act registered patents that are deemed standard patents;
- standard patents based on existing1949 Act patents; or
- standard patents based on patents granted pursuant to an existing application for a 1949 Act patent.

Revocation and putting validity in issue[66] (ss 49, 91 and 101 Patents Ordinance)

The provisions of s 49 of the *Patents Ordinance* apply to all transitional standard patents.

The provisions of ss 91 and 101 of the *Patents Ordinance* apply to

- existing registered 1977 Act patents which are deemed standard patents;
- standard patents based on existing 1977 Act patents; and

- patents based on patents granted pursuant to published 1977 Act patent applications, whether under the normal or alternative procedures.

The provisions of ss 91 and 101 do not apply to

- existing 1949 Act registered patents that are deemed standard patents;
- standard patents granted under the transitional provisions that are based on existing 1949 Act patents; or
- standard patents based on patents granted pursuant to an existing application for a 1949 Act patent.

Thus, under the provisions of ss 91 and 101, the courts in Hong Kong cannot revoke a 1949 Act patent.

Revocation in prescribed opposition proceedings[67] (s 44 Patents Ordinance)

These provisions apply to

- standard patents based on existing 1977 Act patents; and
- patents granted pursuant to a published application for a 1977 Act patent, whether under the normal or alternative procedures.

These provisions do not apply to

- existing registered 1949 Act or 1977 Act patents that are deemed to be standard patents;
- standard patents based on existing 1949 Act patents; or
- standard patents based on patents granted pursuant to an existing application for a 1949 Act patent.

However, these provisions, specifically modified,[68] will apply to such 1949 Act patents. Thus, if the corresponding 1949 Act patent is revoked in the United Kingdom pursuant to revocation proceedings in respect of the 1949 Act patent pursuant to the 1977 Act, then application can be made by any person to the Registrar for a revocation order based on the fact that such patent has been revoked in the United Kingdom.

Compulsory licensing of a standard patent[69] *(ss 64-67 Patents Ordinance)*

These provisions apply, as modified, to existing registered 1977 Act patents that are deemed standard patents. The provisions are modified to state that the right to apply for a compulsory licence will arise three years after the commencement date, namely after 27 June 2000, rather than three years after grant.[70] Thus existing registered patents will, after the three-year grace period, be subject to the compulsory licensing provisions.

The provisions apply without modification to standard patents granted under the transitional provisions based on

- existing 1977 Act patents; or
- patents granted pursuant to a published application for a 1977 Act patent, whether under normal or alternative procedures.

Due to the fact that all 1949 Act patents will expire by June 1998 these provisions will not apply to deemed standard patents or standard patents granted under the transitional provisions that are based on existing 1949 Act patents or existing applications for 1949 Act patents.

Government use of a standard and short-term patent[71] *(ss 68-72 Patents Ordinance)*

The government use provisions of the new law apply to all transitional patents, ie standard patents granted or patents deemed to be standard under the transitional provisions, including existing registered patents.

The government use provisions in force prior to the commencement date of the *Intellectual Property (World Trade Organization Amendments) Ordinance* will continue to apply to acts done before that date.[72]

Nature of a patent and changes to the proprietor[73] *(ss 50-54 Patents Ordinance)*

These provisions apply to all transitional patents, ie existing registered patents deemed to be standard patents and standard patents granted under the transitional provisions.

Language[74] (s 104 Patents Ordinance)

The language provisions of the *Patents Ordinance* relating to the authentic text and the language of proceedings apply to existing registered patents that are deemed standard patents and standard patents granted under the transitional provisions.

The provisions relating to the language of proceedings in respect of existing registered patents are modified to provide that the language of proceedings for applications under the *Registration of Patents Ordinance* will be the language of proceedings for purposes of the new law.[75]

The translation requirements are the same for standard patent applications under the transitional provisions, except that data to be provided in both languages is modified in respect of applications based on existing 1949 Act and 1977 Act patents and patents granted pursuant to existing applications for a 1949 Act patent. This on the basis that only the language requirements of ss 23-27 of the *Patents Ordinance* will apply. It seems, however, that the title of the invention must appear in both English and Chinese.[76]

Register and search facilities[77] (s 51 Patents Ordinance)

The requirements relating to the maintenance of the register and the search facilities apply to all transitional standard patents, ie existing registered patents that are deemed standard patents and standard patents granted under the transitional provisions.

Summary

The new law introduces new provisions for the grant of patents in Hong Kong. On commencement of the new law, proprietors of patents registered under the old law or of patents or patent applications which could have been registered under the old law will have to assess what action needs to be taken under the new law to ensure appropriate patent protection for their inventions in Hong Kong.

In all but a few cases there will be less time to take action under the new law. In summary

- Under the old law: a patent could be registered at any time up to five years after grant or taking effect in the United Kingdom;

- Under the new law: application must be made within six months after publication of the patent application in the designated patent office; and
- Under the transitional provisions: applications must be filed within the set time periods after the commencement date. These time periods are set by *Transitional Rules.*

The transitional provisions provide for the continued protection under the new law of the following categories of patents and patent applications:

- Existing 1949 or 1977 Act registered patents, being patents registered under the old law and in force on the commencement date, are automatically deemed standard patents. Action by the proprietor is not required but it would be advisable to check that the existing registered patent is entered on the register and that the particulars are correct.
- Pending applications for registration under the repealed Ordinance, being applications made under the old law pending registration at the commencement date, will continue to be processed under the old law and will then be considered existing registered patents and accordingly become deemed standard patents. The applicant for registration must comply with the requirements of the old law.
- Existing 1949 or 1977 Act patents, being patents granted by the United Kingdom Patent Office prior to the commencement date, capable of being registered under the old law, but not, in fact, so registered can be used as the basis for a standard patent application under the transitional provisions of the new law. A proprietor of such a patent must apply for the grant of a standard patent under the new law before 27 June 1998[78] or before the end of the five-year term following grant of the existing patent.
- Published 1977 Act patent applications, being published applications for 1977 Act patents pending in the United Kingdom Patent Office or the European Patent Office at the commencement date. The patents, which may be granted pursuant to these applications, must have been capable of being registered under the *Registration of Patents Ordinance*. This term also covers patents granted pursuant to that application after the commencement date. These applications and patents can be

used as the basis for a standard patent application under the transitional provisions of the new law. Application for a standard patent in respect of a published application must be made before 27 December 1998[79] or, if the patent is granted by the United Kingdom Patent Office before 27 June 1998,[80] within six months after the date of such grant.

- Existing applications for a 1949 Act patent, being existing applications for a patent under the 1949 Act still pending before the United Kingdom Patent Office at the commencement date. Patents granted pursuant to that application after the commencement date could be used as the basis for a standard patent application under the transitional provisions of the new law. Application for a standard patent under this category must be made within six months of the grant of the patent in the United Kingdom, provided such grant occurs after 27 June 1997. In no case can an application be made after the patent has expired in the United Kingdom.

The new law sets out the method of obtaining protection in Hong Kong for each category and sets out those parts of the new law, which will apply to each category.

Notes

1 Section 15(6) *Patents Ordinance.*

2 Sections 8 and 15(6).

3 See Chapter 2.

4 See Chapter 2.

5 See Chapter 2.

6 Section 127 1977 Act.

7 Section 11 *Patents (Transitional Arrangements) Rules.*

8 Section 3 *Patents (Transitional Arrangements) Rules.*

9 Section 3(3) *Patents (Transitional Arrangements) Rules.*

10 Section 13 *Patents (Transitional Arrangements) Rules.*

11 Section 3(3) *Patents (Transitional Arrangements) Rules.*

12 Section 10 *Patents (Transitional Arrangements) Rules.*

13 Section 13 *Patents (Transitional Arrangements) Rules.*

14 Section 13 *Patents (Transitional Arrangements) Rules.*

15 Section 14 *Patents (Transitional Arrangements) Rules.*

16 Section 4 *Patents (Transitional Arrangements) Rules.*

17 Section 5 *Patents (Transitional Arrangements) Rules.*

18 Section 5(3) *Patents (Transitional Arrangements) Rules.*

19 Section 6 *Patents (Transitional Arrangements) Rules.*

20 Section 6 *Patents (Transitional Arrangements) Rules.*

21 The time period for filing an application for a standard patent based on an existing 1949 or 1977 Act patent is prescribed in s 6 *Patents (Transitional Arrangements) Rules* as 12 months after the commencement date.

22 Part I Schedule 2 *Patents (Transitional Arrangements) Rules.*

23 Section 6 (4) and Schedule 2 *Patents (Transitional Arrangements) Rules.*

24 Sections 7 and 8 *Patents (Transitional Arrangements) Rules.*

25 The time period for filing a published application for a 1977 Act patent is prescribed in s 7 in the *Patents (Transitional Arrangements) Rules* as 18 months after the commencement date.

26 The time period for filing a published application for a 1977 Act patent is prescribed in s 7 in the *Patents (Transitional Arrangements) Rules* as 18 months after the commencement date.

27 Section 7 and Part I Schedule 3 *Patents (Transitional Arrangements) Rules.*

28 The time period for grant of a patent granted pursuant to a published application for a 1977 Act patent to allow use of the alternative procedure is prescribed by s 8 of the *Patents (Transitional Arrangements) Rules* as 12 months after the commencement date.

29 Section 8 *Patents (Transitional Arrangements) Rules.*

30 Part I Schedule 4 *Patents (Transitional Arrangements) Rules.*

31 Section 9 *Patents (Transitional Arrangements) Rules.*

32 The time period for filing an application for a standard patent based on an existing 1949 patent is prescribed in the *Patents (Transitional Arrangements) Rules* as six months after the grant of the patent.

33 Part 1 Schedule 5 *Patents (Transitional Arrangements) Rules.*

34 Sections 15-27 *Patents Ordinance.*

35 Sections 3-9 and Part I of Schedules 2-5 *Patents (Transitional Arrangements) Rules.*

36 Sections 12 to 22 of the *Patents Ordinance.*

37 Part I Schedule 3 item (f) *Patents (Transitional Arrangements) Rules.*

38 Sections 33-35 *Patents Ordinance.*

39 Para 1 Part II Schedule 3 *Patents (Transitional Arrangements) Rules.*

40 Section 12 *Patents Ordinance.*

41 Section 6 *Patents (Transitional Arrangements) Rules.*

42 Section 8 *Patents (Transitional Arrangements) Rules.*

43 Section 9 *Patents (Transitional Arrangements) Rules.*

44 Section 7 *Patents (Transitional Arrangements) Rules.*

45 Section 38 *Patents Ordinance.*

46 Sections 3-9 and Schedules 1-5 *Patents (Transitional Arrangements) Rules.*

47 Section 39 *Patents Ordinance.*

48 Section 4 *Patents (Transitional Arrangements) Rules.*

49 See Part III Schedule 2, Part II Schedule 3 and Part II Schedule 4.

50 See Part II Schedule 2 and Part II Schedule 5.

51 Sections 57-61 *Patents Ordinance.*

52 Section 61(1) *Patents Ordinance.*

53 Sections 80-83 *Patents Ordinance.*

54 Section 157 *Patents Ordinance* and Section 3-9 and Schedules 1-5 *Patents (Transitional Arrangements) Rules.*

55 Section 157 *Patents Ordinance.*

56 Section 88 *Patents Ordinance.*

57 Para 1 Part II Schedule 3 *Patents (Transitional Arrangements) Rules.*

58 Section 46 *Patents Ordinance.*

59 Section 43 *Patents Ordinance.*

60 Section 11 *Patents (Transitional Arrangements) Rules.*

61 Section 31 *Patents Ordinance.*

62 Section 31 *Patents Ordinance.*

63 Sections 93-97 *Patents Ordinance.*

64 Section 12 *Patents (Transitional Arrangements) Rules.*

65 Section 100 *Patents Ordinance.*

66 Sections 49, 91 and 101 *Patents Ordinance.*

67 Section 44 *Patents Ordinance.*

68 Section 11 *Patents (Transitional Arrangements) Rules.*

69 Sections 64 -67 *Patents Ordinance.*

70 Section 3(2) and Part II Schedule 1 *Patents (Transitional Arrangements) Rules.*

71 Sections 68-72 *Patents Ordinance.*

72 Section 156 *Patents Ordinance.*

73 Sections 50-54 *Patents Ordinance.*

74 Section 104 *Patents Ordinance.*

75 Para 2 Part I Schedule 1 *Patents (Transitional Arrangements) Rules.*

76 See Form P5A(TRA) as published.

77 Section 51 *Patents Ordinance*.

78 The period is within 12 months after commencement date.

79 The period is within 18 months after commencement date.

80 The period is six months after grant if the patent is granted within 12 months after the commencement date.

6 Important Practical Aspects of the Patent Law

This chapter will highlight particular aspects of the new law that have practical significance and set out some of the key dates that may trigger action or which are due dates for taking action.

Making an Application for a Standard Patent under the New Law

There are a number of factors that will come into play when making an application under the new law and some of these are highlighted below.

Choice of patent office

One factor is the choice of patent office. The new law provides that a standard patent can be granted after the registration of a patent by a designated patent office. The *Patents Ordinance* gives the Chief Executive-in-Council the power to designate patent offices for the purposes of the Ordinance.[1] The Ordinance also provides that application for a standard patent cannot be made in respect of an application published by a patent office before that office is designated a designated patent office.[2]

This means that a standard patent application under the new law can be made in respect of all applications published by a designated patent office after designation by the Chief Executive-in-Council or the commencement date, whichever is later.

The Governor-in-Council designated the Chinese Patent Office, the European Patent Office in respect of European patents (UK) and United Kingdom Patent Office with effect from the commencement date.[3] Standard patent applicants in Hong Kong will therefore have a choice in selecting which designated patent office to use as the basis for applying for a patent in Hong Kong.

It is important to note that all three patent offices

- provide strong and well-respected patents;
- have compatible patent laws, particularly as regards the type of inventions capable of being patented and the level of patentability; and
- are Designated Offices and Receiving Offices for the purposes of the PCT. In addition the European Patent Office and the Chinese Patent Office and formerly the United Kingdom Patent Office are international searching authorities for the purposes of the PCT. This means that all offices have been recognised for this purpose by the members of the PCT.

The decision of which designated patent to select as the basis for the grant in Hong Kong will depend on a number of factors, including marketing considerations and cost effectiveness. In most instances, the decision will be primarily a commercial one based on the circumstances of each application.

The main advantage of a registration system is that once a patent is granted by a designated patent office, no further substantive examination is required before grant of a patent in Hong Kong. Invention owners can choose from among three offices. Thus a person who wishes to exploit an invention in Hong Kong and Europe only will choose the United Kingdom or the European Patent Office. Likewise, a person wishing to exploit the invention in China and Hong Kong will choose the Chinese Patent Office.

Language

Another factor is the question of language.[4] An application in Hong Kong can be in English or Chinese. The language of the application in Hong Kong will be the language of the proceedings before the Registrar. The language of proceedings can be changed, subject to directions by the Registrar as to translations, and can be different from that of the designated patent office.

The authentic text of the standard patent specification or the standard patent application will be the text of the corresponding designated patent or designated patent application in the language of proceedings before the designated patent office.

This will apply even if the language of proceedings in Hong Kong is different from that in the designated patent office. This basic rule is subject to special provisions dealing with discrepancies between a translation and the authentic text where such translation confers a narrower protection and where the language of the authentic text is not in English or Chinese.

The *Patent (General) Rules*[5] provide that, on application for a standard or short-term patent, certain specified data are to be provided in both official languages. This data is the abstract and title of the invention. In addition, if the name of the applicant and the inventor are not in the Roman alphabet, then they must also be translated in the Roman alphabet. Such requirements are undoubtedly of benefit to potential users of the system for search purposes. Translations of documents filed with an application, including the description claims and drawings as contained in the designated patent application and in the patent specification when granted, will not be required.

As outlined above, if the description claims and drawings as contained in the designated patent application and the patent specification when granted are in one of the official languages, it will not be necessary to translate them into the other. Nor do the Patent Rules require an applicant to file a translation of the specification into the language of the proceedings, even if it is in a language other than one of the official languages.

Thus if the application for a standard patent is based on an European patent (UK) where the language of proceedings was in German or French, only the title of the invention and the abstract need be translated into both English and Chinese. The authentic text will be the German or French text. This will assist applicants, but only time will tell whether users are prejudiced.

In summary, the language of proceedings can be either English or Chinese. The choice of language in Hong Kong can be different from the language of proceedings in the designated patent office. The abstract and title of the invention must be given in both official languages and documents in support of title that are in a language other than one of the official languages must be translated into the language of the proceedings. Apart from these requirements, no other documents need be translated on application, whether from one official language to another or from a non-official language to an official language.

Language, although having some impact on the choice of designated patent office, may not be a major factor because the language provisions are not too onerous under the new law. Applicants have the flexibility of choosing the language of proceedings, irrespective of the language of proceedings in the designated patent office.

Key Dates under the New Law

There are a number of key dates under the new law. Some of these dates act as a trigger for action to be taken within a specified time, for example, commencement date, date of publication of designated patent application, etc. Others operate as the anniversary date on which action is to be taken, eg deemed date of filing for renewal of a standard patent. A number of these key dates are highlighted below. In addition, the key dates for taking certain action are separately highlighted.

The commencement date of the new law

Once the *Patents Ordinance* was enacted, it became necessary for the owners of inventions to assess their patent and patent application portfolios to see what steps needed to be taken to obtain patent protection in Hong Kong, whether under the old law, the new law or the transitional provisions of the new law.

In making such an assessment, the commencement date was key in deciding whether to

- register under the old law before the new law actually came into operation;
- make an application for a standard patent under the new law once the new law came into operation; or
- make an application for a standard patent under the transitional provisions of the new law after the new law came into operation.

The significance of the commencement date in deciding what action to take to obtain patent protection in Hong Kong is as follows:

- Application for registration under the old law could be made up to the day before the commencement date and still be processed and registered as of the date prior to the commencement date under the old law.
- All existing registered patents, ie patents registered under the current law and in force in the United Kingdom on the

commencement date, were deemed standard patents on the commencement date and automatically transferred to the new register.

- Patent applications published by a designated patent office after the commencement date can be the basis for an application for grant of a standard patent under the new law, whether or not the patent application in the designated patent office had been made before or after the commencement date.
- Standard patent applications based on patents granted or published before the commencement date can only be made if they fall within the transitional provisions.[6]
- Under the transitional provisions, a standard patent application can be made based on a patent granted before the commencement date under the United Kingdom *Patents Acts* of 1949 or 1977 (including European patents (UK)), which take effect under that Act.
- Under the transitional provisions a standard patent application can be made based on a patent application that has been published prior to the commencement date and which could be granted or take effect under the United Kingdom *Patents Act* 1997.
- Under the transitional provisions, a standard patent application can be made based on a patent granted after the commencement date pursuant to an existing application for a 1949 Act patent.

Date of publication of the designated patent application in the designated patent office

A key date is the date of publication of the designated patent application by the designated patent office, which occurs after the commencement date. It is the trigger date for making a standard patent application under the new law. A request to record the designated patent application must be made within six months after that date.[7]

Date of publication of the request to record in Hong Kong

The date of publication of the request to record is the date on which rights arise, including the right to bring an action and claim damages in respect of any such rights. Such action can only be brought after the standard patent has been granted.[8]

Date of grant of the designated patent

The date of grant of the designated patent is the trigger date for the second stage of the application procedure, when the first stage has been complied with. A request to register the designated patent and grant of patent must be filed within six months after that date.[9]

Deemed filing date of standard patent application

The deemed filing date is the date of filing in the designated patent office of the corresponding designated patent application. This date is the deemed filing date of the standard patent application for the purposes of the *Patents Ordinance* after the patent is granted.[10] The deemed filing date is the key date for the purposes of, *inter alia*

- *the term:* the term commences on the deemed date of filing;
- *renewal of the standard patent after grant:* renewal is required on the anniversary of the deemed date of filing falling three years after grant and thereafter annually;
- *establishing novelty:* the state-of-the-art is assessed as at the deemed date of filing if priority is not claimed; and
- *establishing the right to a patent:* in the case of an independently created patent, the right to the patent, if priority is not claimed, belongs to the proprietor of the patent with the first deemed filing date in any of the designated patent offices or the date of filing in Hong Kong Patents Registry of a short-term patent respectively.

Date of filing the designated patent application

For the purposes of a standard patent application the date of filing the designated patent application is the key date in respect of maintaining a standard patent application. The standard patent application must be maintained on the anniversary of the date of filing the designated patent application, falling on the expiry of the fifth year after publication of the request to record and thereafter annually.

Date of grant of the standard patent

The date of grant of the standard patent is, of course, a key date and it is a trigger date for a number of matters. It is a key date for

- rights which arise from that date;
- renewal, which is required on the first anniversary of the filing date falling after the expiry of the period of three years after grant; and
- grant of a compulsory licence, which can be applied for at any time after the period of three years after grant.

Date of amendment in the designated patent office of the standard patent specification

If the specification of the corresponding patent granted by the designated patent office is amended in prescribed opposition or revocation proceedings, the proprietor is required to notify the Registrar within three months after the date of amendment in the designated patent office.[11]

If the proprietor files particulars of such amendment the Registrar must file these. If the proprietor fails to apply within the set time period, then application can still be made to the court under s 46 of the *Patents Ordinance*. The court does, however, have discretion under this section and failure to file particulars of an amendment within the due time may be taken into account by the court in deciding whether to allow the amendment or to allow it subject to conditions.

The *trigger date* for proprietors who amend their patents in prescribed opposition or revocation proceedings before the designated patent office is the date of amendment in the designated patent office or the date of grant of the standard patent, whichever is the later. The key dates are

- the date of the order of amendment or grant of the standard patent, if later; and
- the end of the three-month period within which details of the amendment must be filed in the Hong Kong Patents Registry.

Key Dates in Relation to an Application for a Standard Patent

Some of the key dates in relation to an application and a standard patent when granted are highlighted below.

Key dates for registering under the old law

The trigger date for registering under the old law was the date of grant of the 1949 Act and 1977 Act patent. Application had to be made within five years of grant.

The key dates were, therefore, the date of grant or taking effect of the 1949 Act or 1977 Act patent in the United Kingdom and the date falling five years after that grant. Application for registration under the old law could not be made on or after the commencement date.

Key dates for making a standard patent application under the new law

There are three main trigger dates for making a standard patent application under the new law. These are set out as follows:

First trigger date

The first trigger date for making an application under the new law is publication of the designated patent application in the designated patent office after the commencement date. Application must be made within six months after that date.

The key dates for applicants in Hong Kong are the

- date of publication of the designated patent application; and
- the date falling six months after that date.

Application must be made during the period beginning and ending with these dates.

Second potential trigger date

The second potential trigger date is the anniversary of the date of filing the designated patent application. This falls after the expiry of five years following publication of the request to record. The application must be maintained if it is to be kept pending.

Third trigger date

The third trigger date, if the request to record is published, is the date of grant of the designated patent. Application must be made within six months after that date.

The key dates at the second stage are therefore the

- date of grant of the designated patent by the designated patent office; and
- the date six months after that date.

Application must be made within the period beginning or ending with this period.

Key dates for making an application for a standard patent and for the life of the patent

The key dates in Hong Kong for making an application and maintaining it after grant are as follows:

- Date of filing the application in the designated patent office, which is considered the deemed filing date of a standard patent application in Hong Kong.
- Date of priority claimed and accorded in the designated patent office which, if claimed in Hong Kong on application, is the accorded date of priority in Hong Kong.
- Publication date of the designated patent application in the designated patent office, as the application in Hong Kong must be filed within six months after that date.
- Date of entry into the national phase of an international application in the designated patent office, as the application in Hong Kong must be filed within six months after the date of publication or notification of such entry.
- Date of publication of the request to record in Hong Kong, being the date on which rights arise and also the right to bring an action and claim damages in respect of any such rights after the standard patent has been granted.
- The anniversary of the date of filing of the designated patent application falling five years after the date of publication of the request to record and annually on that date thereafter, being the dates on which the application is required to be maintained.
- Date of grant of the corresponding designated patent by the designated patent office, as the application at the second stage must be made in Hong Kong within six months after that date.
- Date of grant of the standard patent, being the date
  (i) on which the right to bring action arises;
  (ii) from which the three-year period before first renewal is calculated; and

(iii) from which the three-year period before a compulsory licence can be granted is calculated.

- Deemed date of filing of the standard patent application, ie date of filing the corresponding designated patent application being, *inter alia*
  (i) the renewal date of the patent, being the anniversary of that date first falling three years after date of grant and thereafter annually; and
  (ii) the date from which the term is calculated.
- Date of amendment of the corresponding designated patent in the designated patent office after prescribed opposition or revocation proceedings, as the order of such amendment must be filed with the Hong Kong Patents Registry within a set period if such amendment is to automatically apply and be recorded in Hong Kong.
- Date of assignment, charge, licence or other transaction affecting the patent or the patent application is made, as application to record this must be made with the Hong Kong Patents Registry within six months of that date to avoid loss of certain rights in the patent.

Key Dates in Relation to the Transitional Provisions

The following are the key dates for the various categories of patents dealt with under the transitional provisions.[12]

Existing 1949 or 1977 Act registered patents

The key date for existing 1949 or 1977 Act registered patents is the commencement date. All 1949 Act or 1977 Act patents registered under the old law and in force on the commencement date were transferred to the new register and were deemed to be standard patents.

The commencement date is also a key date because

- rights under the new law will arise;
- renewal will be required on the anniversary of the date of filing in the United Kingdom or the European Patent Office from the expiry of the third year after the commencement date; and

- compulsory licences can be granted at any time after three years following the commencement date.

Pending applications for registration under the repealed Ordinance

The commencement date is the key date for applications made under the current law pending registration at the commencement date. The application will continue to be processed under the current law and then transferred to the new register as an existing registered patent.

Existing 1949 or 1977 Act patents

The commencement date is the trigger date for existing 1949 Act and 1977 Act patents as application must be made for a standard patent under the transitional provisions within 12 months after the commencement date (that is, before 27 June 1998), or before the end of a term of five years after grant of the existing patent, whichever is the earlier.

On grant of a standard patent based on an existing 1949 Act or 1977 Act patent, the key dates are the same as for a standard patent granted under the new law.

Published applications for a 1977 Act patent

The commencement date is the trigger date for published applications for a 1977 Act patent, as application must be made

- under normal procedures within 18 months after the commencement date, that is 27 December 1998; or
- under the alternative procedures, ie if the patent is granted within 12 months after the commencement date (that is 27 June 1998), then within six months after the date of such grant.

Thus the key dates for the normal procedures are

- the commencement date; and
- the 18-month period after commencement date within which application must be made.

The key dates for the alternative procedures are

- the commencement date;
- the date of grant by the United Kingdom Patent Office within 12 months after the commencement date; and
- the period of six months after the date of grant by the United Kingdom Patent Office.

On publication of the request to record or on the grant of the standard patent the key dates are the same as for a standard patent granted under the new law.

Existing applications for a 1949 Act patent

The key date for the existing applications for a 1949 Act patent is the commencement date as the application must still be pending at that date. The trigger date is the grant of the 1949 Act patent by the United Kingdom Patent Office after the commencement date, as the standard patent application under this category must be made within six months of the grant of the patent in the United Kingdom.

On the grant of a standard patent based on a patent granted pursuant to an existing application for a 1949 Act patent, the key dates are the same as for a standard patent granted under the new law as modified by the transitional provisions, to reflect the fact that all 1949 Act patents will have expired by 1 June 1998.

Applications to the Court or the Registrar

The responsibility of the Registrar under the *Patents Ordinance* falls into three areas. Firstly, to receive and process applications for standard patents and short-term patents and to grant standard patents and short-term patents. Secondly, to maintain a register of patent applications and patents granted and to record renewals and changes to patents. Thirdly, to make the register and other information on patents and patent applications available to the public. Thus all patent applications are made to the Registrar and any changes to the register or the patent specification must be recorded with the Registrar.

In the main, questions relating to the validity and ownership of a patent are to be determined by the court. The *Patents Ordinance* defines the court as being the High Court in Hong Kong. There is a right of appeal from the Court of First Instance to the Court of Appeal. There are however some questions, which can be considered and determined by the Registrar, without application being made to the court but subject to appeal to the court. Highlighted below are those questions that can be determined only by the court; others that can be determined by the court or the Registrar; and others that the Registrar can determine, subject, in some cases, to a right to refer the question to the court for decision. All cases determined by the Registrar are subject to appeal to the court. The court has the power to determine any question, to make any order or exercise any power that could have been made by the Registrar.[13]

Matters to be determined by the court

Only the court has the power to determine the following questions:

- Amendment of a patent specification after grant except in certain limited cases (s 46 *Patents Ordinance*);
- Application for rectification of the register by a person aggrieved by an entry on the register (s 53 *Patents Ordinance*);
- Determination of questions of entitlement to a patent after grant of the patent (s 55 *Patents Ordinance*);
- Application for compensation by an employee for inventions made by an employee (s 58 *Patents Ordinance*);
- Application for a compulsory licence for a standard patent (s 64 *Patents Ordinance*);
- Referral of a dispute in relation to Government use of a patent (s 72 *Patents Ordinance*);
- Proceedings for patent infringement (s 80 *Patents Ordinance*);
- Proceedings in relation to rights conferred by publication of a standard patent (s 88 *Patents Ordinance*);
- Application for a certificate of contested validity of a patent (s 84 *Patents Ordinance*);
- Proceedings for relief in relation to threats of groundless infringement proceedings (s 89 *Patents Ordinance*);
- Applications for a declaration of non-infringement (s 90 *Patents Ordinance*);
- Revocation of a patent, except in certain limited cases (s 91 *Patents Ordinance*); and
- The validity of a patent in those proceedings in which validity may be put in issue (s 101 *Patents Ordinance*).

Any finding or order of the court is subject to appeal to the Court of Appeal.

Matters to be determined by the court or the Registrar

The court or the Registrar may determine, before grant of a standard patent, the question of who has the right to apply for a standard patent (ss 13 and 42 *Patents Ordinance*). If application is made to the Registrar, he may refer the case to the court or may hear the case subject to appeal to the court.

Matters to be recorded by the Registrar

The Registrar is required to record the following, without application to the court:

- Amendments to a standard patent application or a short-term patent application before grant (ss 31 and 120 *Patents Ordinance*);
- Amendments to a standard patent on filing a verified copy of the amendment to the designated patent after amendment of the designated patent in prescribed opposition or revocation proceedings, within three months of the date of amendment in the designated patent office or the date of grant of the standard patent, whichever is the later (s 43 *Patents Ordinance*); and
- Record the revocation of a standard patent on the filing by the patent proprietor of a verified copy of a revocation order of a designated patent issued by the designated patent office after revocation in prescribed opposition or revocation proceedings and advertising this fact (s 44 *Patents Ordinance*).

The Registrar is required to record these matters and has no discretion to refuse to record these on the register unless there are discrepancies in the documents filed.

Matters to be determined by the Registrar subject to appeal to the court

The Registrar has the right, without application being made to the court, to:

- Allow restoration of rights, restoration of an application for a standard patent and restoration of a patent to the register (ss 29, 34 ,40, 123 and 127 *Patents Ordinance*);
- Refuse to register a request to record or to grant a standard patent or a short-term patent on the grounds that it is contrary to *ordre public* or morality (ss 37 and 124 *Patents Ordinance*);
- Make a finding, on request, relating to mention of an inventor in a patent granted for such invention (s 45 *Patents Ordinance*); and
- Correct any errors in any patent application specification or any document filed with such application (s 146 *Patents Ordinance*).

Before determining these questions, the Registrar must give any party a right to be heard.[14] Any decision of the Registrar is subject to appeal to the court.[15]

Matters to be determined by the Registrar, subject to his right to refer to the court

The Registrar has the right, without application to the court, to:

- Revoke a standard patent on application by a person other than the proprietor of the patent where the designated patent has been revoked by the designated patent office after prescribed opposition or revocation proceedings (ss 44 (4) and (5) *Patents Ordinance*);
- Accept an offer to surrender a patent (s 48 *Patents Ordinance*); and
- Revoke a patent on application by any person on the ground that the patent is contrary to *ordre public* or morality (s 49 *Patents Ordinance*).

In such cases the Registrar may, at any stage of the proceedings, refer the case to the court or proceed to hear the case.[16] In certain cases he must give other interested parties the right to oppose the application. Before determining these questions, the Registrar must give any party a right to be heard.[17] Any decision of the Registrar may be appealed to the court.[18]

Notes

1 Section 8 *Patents Ordinance.*

2 Section 15(6) *Patents Ordinance.*

3 Patents (Designation of Patent Offices) Notice.

4 Sections 104-106 *Patents Ordinance.*

5 Section 56 Patents (General) Rules.

6 See Chapter 5.

7 Section 15 *Patents Ordinance.*

8 Section 88 *Patents Ordinance.*

9 Section 23 *Patents Ordinance.*

10 Section 38 *Patents Ordinance.*

11 Section 43 *Patents Ordinance* and s 35 *Patents (General) Rules.*

12 See Chapter 5.

13 Section 132 *Patents Ordinance.*

14 Section 135 *Patents Ordinance.*

15 Section 130 *Patents Ordinance.*

16 Section 133 *Patents Ordinance.*

17 Section 135 *Patents Ordinance.*

18 Section 130 *Patents Ordinance.*

7 The Patents Ordinance Explained

As explained in Chapter 4 the *Patents Ordinance* is divided into Parts I to XIX and has two Schedules.

The Patents Ordinance	
Part I	Preliminary
Part II	Applications for Standard Patents
Part III	Provisions as to Applications for Standard Patents before Grant
Part IV	Provisions as to Patents after Grant
Part V	Property in Patents and Applications; Registration
Part VI	Employees' Inventions
Part VII	Contracts as to Patented Products etc.
Part VIII	Compulsory Licences for Standard Patents
Part IX	Government Use of Patented Inventions
Part X	The Effects of Patent and Patent Application
Part XI	Infringement
Part XII	Revocation of Patents
Part XIII	General Provisions as to Amendment of Patents and Patent Applications
Part XIV	Language of Proceedings; Authentic Text
Part XV	Short-term Patents
Part XVI	Miscellaneous
Part XVII	Offences
Part XVIII	Administrative Provisions
Part XIX	Repeals and Transitional Arrangements
Schedule 1	Paris Convention countries and WTO members, territories and areas
Schedule2	Section 7G Registration of Patents Ordinance

Part I: Preliminary (Sections 1-9)

Section 2 sets out the general interpretation provisions. Some of the main definitions are set out below:

- The term *standard patent* refers to a patent granted under Part II;
- The term *short-term patent* refers to a short-term patent granted under Part XV;
- The term *request to record* refers to the request under s 15 to record a designated patent application;
- The term *request for registration and grant* means the request under s 23 for the registration of the designated patent and the grant of the standard patent at the second stage;
- The meaning of the term *date of filing* depends on the document referred, namely:
  - *date of filing request to record* is the date of filing accorded to it by the Registrar under s 17; and
  - *date of filing an application for a standard patent* is the date accorded to the filing of the request to record;
- *Date of filing a designated patent application* is the date so specified in the designated patent application;
- The *court* means the Court of First Instance of Hong Kong;
- Reference to an *international application* means an application for a patent made under the PCT;
- *Opposition or revocation proceedings* means proceedings in relation to the designated patent which provides for revocation or amendment in immediate post grant proceedings.[1] These have been defined in the *Patents Rules* as the opposition proceedings in the European Patent Office and immediate post grant proceedings in the Chinese Patent Office.

Section 3 provides that the term *application for a standard patent* refers to the application from the date of filing the request to record up to grant. This expression does not refer to the patent once granted.

Section 4 defines a *designated patent* as the patent granted by the designated patent office, a *designated patent application* as an application published by a designated patent office or an *international application* which has been published and validly entered the national phase in the designated patent office. References in the *Patents*

Ordinance to a *corresponding designated patent application or designated patent* are references to the designated patent application or designated patent on which the application in Hong Kong was based.

Section 5 defines the term *published*. The meaning depends on the context. In general the term *published* means that information has been made available to the public anywhere in the world. *Published* under the *Patents Ordinance* means any document which can be inspected as of right in Hong Kong. This section further specifies the meaning of the term in relation to publication by the designated patent office and in other contexts.

Section 6 defines a patent as including both a standard patent and a short-term patent. It also defines certain other terms and references. In particular, s 6(4) states that reference to an *invention being worked in Hong Kong* includes reference to the invention being imported for the purpose of putting the product on the market or stocking it for that purpose.

Section 7 makes it clear that filing a document will only be complete when the fee is paid and a document will not be considered as filed until the fee is so paid. This is subject to some exceptions most notably on filing an application for a patent when a date of filing can be accorded without payment of the fee.

Section 8 gives the power to the Chief Executive-in-Council to designate a patent office for the purposes of the *Patents Ordinance*.[2]

Section 9 contains special provisions where an invention is covered by more than one granted patent. These provisions state that any use which would not be considered infringement of one patent will not be considered as infringement of the other patent. This provision is necessary because the patent system allows patents to be granted after formality examination only. It is, therefore, possible for more than one patent to be granted for the same invention.

Part II: Applications for Standard Patents (Sections 10-30)

This Part deals with the application procedures for a *standard patent*.

Section 10 describes the application procedures. **Section 11** expressly states that the Registrar is only required to examine the application as to formal requirements and not as to substance.

Sections 12 to 14 set out who may apply for a standard patent and for the determination of questions before grant on application to the court or to the Registrar.

Sections 15 to 22 contain the detailed provisions for making the application at the first stage including the documents to be filed, the minimum requirements for obtaining a filing date, the detail of examination by the Registrar and making good any deficiencies in the application, the recording of the request to record and its publication.

Sections 23 to 27 similarly contain the detailed provisions for making the application at the second stage and for the grant and publication of the standard patent .

Sections 28 to 30 contain the provisions to deal with reactivation or restoration where an application is deemed withdrawn because of a failure to comply with a time limit and the effects of restoration.

Part III: Provisions as to Standard Patents before Grant (Sections 31-37)

Sections 31 to 32 and 36 deal with amendments and the withdrawal at the request of the applicant of a standard patent application before grant.

Sections 33 to 35 set out the requirements for the maintenance of a standard patent application and for restoration in the event of failure to maintain and the effects of restoration.

Section 37 gives the Registrar the right to refuse to record or register a request if he considers the subject matter of the patent is not patentable because it is contrary to *ordre public* or morality.

Part IV: Provisions as to Patents after Grant (Sections 38-49)

Sections 38 to 44 deal with certain matters relating to standard patents after grant.

Section 38 defines the meaning of the term *deemed date of filing* after the standard patent has been granted to be the date of filing of the corresponding designated patent application.

Sections 39 to 41 set out the term of the standard patent and provide for renewal and restoration in the event of failure to renew.

Section 42 gives the power to the court or the Registrar to continue to hear after grant any questions referred prior to grant but not determined at the time of grant. This section specifically provides that, if any such questions have not been determined at the time of grant, this will not prevent the standard patent being granted and published.

Sections 43 and 44 contain special provisions allowing amendment and revocation of the standard patent where the corresponding designated patent has been amended or revoked by the designated patent office as a result of prescribed opposition or revocation proceedings in the designated patent office.[3] Such amendment can be made on filing evidence with the Registrar by the proprietor of the standard patent. In addition, in the case of the revocation of the corresponding designated patent in such proceedings application by any person may be made to the Registrar for an order to revoke the standard patent.

Sections 45 to 49 apply to all types of patents and deal with matters relating to the unity of the invention, the inventor and amendments of the specification of the patent.

Section 45 deals with right to the inventor to be named as such in the patent. **Section 46** deals with the general right of the proprietor to apply to the court to amend the specification of the patent after grant and the power of the court to allow any such amendment, subject to any conditions it thinks fit. **Section 47** states that in proceedings no patent may be impugned for lack of unity. **Section 48** deals with the right of the proprietor to give notice to the Registrar to offer to surrender the patent and **section 49** gives power to the Registrar to revoke the patent on application by any person on the grounds that the invention is not patentable because it is contrary to *ordre public* or morality.

Part V: Property in Patents and Applications; Registration (Sections 50-56)

Sections 50 to 56 deal with the nature of a patent and patent application and provide for

- the maintenance of the register;

- public inspection of the register;
- the rectification of the register by the court; and
- other matters relating to the property in patents and applications.

Section 50 provides that a patent and a patent application are personal property and may be dealt with as such. **Section 51** provides for the Registrar to keep a register in accordance with the Rules; for Rules to be made to deal with the registration of patents and applications for patents and transactions and other documents affecting them; and for the provision of copies, on request, of documents registered under these provisions. **Section 52** provides for the priority of documents where application has been made for registration over those where no such application has been made. **Section 53** gives the court the power on application by any person aggrieved to rectify the register. **Section 54** deals with the co-ownership of patents or applications for patents.

Sections 55 and 56 enable application to be made to the court but not the Registrar, to decide questions relating to the person entitled to the patent after the grant of the patent.

Part VI: Employees' Inventions (Sections 57-61)

Sections 57 to 61 govern the provisions relating to employees' inventions, where the employee was mainly employed in Hong Kong at the time of making the invention.

Section 57 sets out entitlement to such inventions as between the employer and the employee.

Sections 58 to 59 allow an employee to apply to the court for compensation in certain circumstances and **section 60** deals with the enforceability of contracts between the employer and employee in relation to such inventions.

Section 61 provides that the provisions of Part VI apply only if the invention is made after the commencement date and if the employee is mainly employed in Hong Kong. If the employee has no main place of employment then the provisions will apply if the employer has a place of business in Hong Kong and if the employee was attached to that place of business.

Part VII: Contracts as to Patented Products and Others (Sections 62-63)

Sections 62 and 63 contain provisions which deal with the avoidance of certain contracts for supply or licensing of a patented product if certain types of restrictions are imposed on that supply or licence and for the determination of parts of contracts in certain circumstances.

Part VIII: Compulsory Licences for Standard Patents (Sections 64-67)

Sections 64 to 67 set out the provisions relating to the grant of a compulsory licence of a standard patent by the court.

Section 64 provides that any person may apply to the court for the grant of such a licence at any time after the expiry of three years from the grant of the patent. The court may grant such licence on such conditions as it thinks fit. This section also sets out the grounds on which such application can be made and the conditions which must be satisfied before the court may order such a licence. **Section 65** gives the court power to extend the licence to customers of the applicant in the circumstances set out. **Section 66** sets out the basis on which the court should exercise its powers under this Part. **Section 67** gives the proprietor of the patent or any other person the right to oppose such licence.

Part IX: Government Use of Patented Inventions (Sections 68-72)

Sections 68 to 72 provide for the government use of patents during a period of extreme urgency subject to payment of reasonable remuneration and for reference of any dispute to the court.

Section 68 gives the Chief Executive-in-Council the power to declare a period of extreme urgency if it is considered necessary in the public interest for maintaining or securing sufficient supplies and services essential to the life of the community.

Section 69 provides that any person duly authorised by the Government may use the invention without the consent of the proprietor during the period of extreme urgency. Such government use must be on terms agreed by the Government and the proprietor. If no such agreement is reached then the terms will fall to be determined by the court. The Government must inform the proprietor of the patent of such use as soon as possible.

Sections 70 and 71 deal with the rights of third parties, ie licensees or assignees who may be affected by such government use and for the payment by the Government of compensation to the proprietor or an exclusive licensee for any loss in profits which may result from such use.

Section 72 allows for any disputes between the Government or any person on the use by the Government of the patented invention or on the terms of such use to be referred to the court. In considering such disputes the court must take into account any benefit which such person may be entitled to receive from the Government and whether the request by the Government for such use by such person on reasonable terms was not met.

Part X: The Effects of a Patent and Patent Application (Sections 73 to 79)

Sections 73 to 79 set out the rights given to the owner of a patent on grant and some matters relating to the interpretation of claims.

Sections 73 and 74 give the proprietor the right to prevent all third parties from making, putting on the market, using or importing a product which is the subject matter of the patent or which is obtained directly from a process which is the subject matter of the patent, without his consent. In addition, the proprietor may prevent the stocking of such product, whether for putting it on the market in Hong Kong or elsewhere, or otherwise. Where the subject matter of the patent is a process then the proprietor has the right to prevent third parties from using the process or offering the process for use in Hong Kong without his consent when the other person knows, or should know because it is obvious in the circumstances, that the use of the process without consent is not allowed. Under **section 74** the proprietor also has the right to prevent third parties from supplying a person in Hong Kong with the means of putting the invention into effect when that person knows, or should know because it is obvious in the circumstances, that the means are suitable and intended for putting that invention into effect in Hong Kong. **Section 75** sets out certain limitations on the rights given to the proprietor. In particular the rights do not extend to non-commercial acts done privately, experimental acts relating to the invention or single extemporaneous preparations under a medical prescription of a medicine

Section 76 sets out the extent of the protection given by a patent or a patent application and the interpretation of the specification. It provides that the specification is to be interpreted as defining a position which combines a fair protection for the proprietor with reasonable degree of certainty for third parties. **Sections 77 to 79** set out the requirements for disclosure and the contents of the claims and the abstract.

Part XI: Infringement (Sections 80-90)

Sections 80 to 90 set out the actions which may be brought by the proprietor of a patent if his rights are infringed and deal with the rights of third parties to continue use begun before the priority date, the bringing of proceedings by co-owners and exclusive licensees, infringement rights on publication of the standard patent and the remedy for groundless threats.

Sections 80 to 82 enables the proprietor of the patent to bring civil proceedings in the court in respect of any infringement of the patent and to request injunctions, damages, delivery up, and other similar remedies. These sections contain provisions which restrict the amount of damages which can be claimed in certain circumstances, give relief if the patent is found partially valid. **Section 83** gives a right to continue use in Hong Kong where such use commenced before the deemed date of filing or the priority date.

Section 84 gives the court the power to give a certificate that the validity of a patent was contested where the court has found the patent to be wholly or partially valid in court proceedings.

Sections 85 and 86 set out the power given to the co-owner of the patent and an exclusive licensee to bring an action for infringement in certain circumstances. **Section 87** provides for limitations on the right of a person who becomes a proprietor or exclusive licensee of a patent to claim damages if such person does not apply to register the particulars of the transaction establishing his right within six months of the date of the transaction.

Section 88 sets out the rights given to the proprietor of a standard patent application on the publication of the request to record. **Section 89** sets out the remedy if groundless threats of infringement are made. **Section 90** allows the court in the circumstances outlined to make a declaration that a certain act does not constitute infringement.

Part XII: Revocation of Patents (Sections 91-101)

Sections 91 to 101 contain the general provisions relating to the right of any person to apply to the court for revocation of a patent. It also sets out the criteria for patentable inventions, matters relating to the priority of standard patent application, the right to a patent and when validity may be put in issue.

This part is dealt with under the following headings:

- General provisions (ss 91 to 92);
- Patentable inventions (ss 93 to 97);
- Priority of standard patent applications (ss 98 to 99);
- The right to a patent (s 100); and
- Putting validity in issue (s 101).

Sections 91 and 92 set out the grounds on which application for revocation can be made. Application can be made by any person. **Section 93** sets out those inventions which are patentable and defines novelty in **sections 94 and 95**, inventive step in **section 96** and industrial application in **section 97. Sections 98 to 99** deal with the establishment of a right to priority in respect of standard patent and the effect of the priority right.

Section 100 provides that the right to a patent belongs to the inventor or his successor in title and contains provisions establishing that in the case of an employee who is an inventor the right is determined in accordance with the law of the place where that person is primarily employed or the place of business of the employer to which the employee is attached. This section also establishes the first to file principle in respect of inventions which are independently created.

Section 101 sets out those proceedings before the court where the validity of a patent may be put in issue.

Part XIII: General Provisions as to Amendment of Patents and Patent Applications (Sections 102 & 103)

Sections 102 and 103 contain provisions relating to the circumstances in which a patent can be amended and states that amendments to patents and patent applications may not include any added matter. Any such amendment will be invalid to the extent that it extends the subject matter of the application as filed.

Part XIV: Language of the Proceedings; Authentic Text (Sections 104-107)

Sections 104 to 107 set out the language requirements for an application for a patent, the language of the proceedings and provides for the authentic text. **Section 104** provides that the application may be made in one of the official languages, ie English or Chinese and provides for Rules[4] to be made to deal with certain matters relating to translations into the language of the proceedings of one or both of the official languages. **Section 105** sets the basic rule that the text in the language of the proceedings is the authentic text. **Section 106** provides special rules for the authentic text of a standard patent and standard patent application. **Section 107** establishes the obvious point that any amendments of the specification must be made in the language of the proceedings.

Part XV: Short-term Patents (Sections 108-129)

Sections 108 to 129 provide for the grant of short-term patents and contains special provisions which apply only to short-term patents.

Section 108 provides that any person may apply for a short-term patent. Special provisions are contained in **section 109** to deal with the claim for a non-prejudicial disclosure and in **sections 110 to 112** to deal with a claim for priority and the effect of such claim in relation to a short-term patent.

Sections 113 to 116 contain the detailed provisions for making a short-term patent application including the documents to be filed, the minimum requirements for obtaining a filing date, the detail of examination by the Registrar and the making good of any deficiencies in the application. **Section 117** expressly provides for the non-examination system by stating that the Registrar is only required to examine the application as to formal requirements and not as to substance. **Section 118** provides for the grant and publication of the short-term patent. **Section 119** contains the special provision which allows an applicant to request at the time of making the application that the grant of the short-term patent be deferred for a period of up to 12 months. **Sections 120 to 122** allow for the amendment and withdrawal of the application on the conditions outlined. **Section 123** contains the provisions applying sections 27 to 30 as amended to deal with reactivation or restoration where an application is deemed withdrawn because of a failure to comply with a time limit. **Section 124** gives power to the Registrar to refuse to grant a short-term patent on the basis that the invention is contrary to *ordre public* or morality. **Section 125** contains the special provisions where the short-term patent application is based on an international application which has designated China. **Sections 126 to 127** set out the term of the short-term patent and provide for renewal and restoration in the event of failure to renew. **Section 128** deals with the disclosure of the specification in a sufficiently clear and complete manner in the case of an invention which requires for its performance the use of a micro-organism and provides that rules may be made for this purpose.[5] **Section 129** contains special provisions dealing with court proceedings involving a short-term patent. In such proceedings the proprietor must establish *prima facie* the validity of a patent and where injunctions are claimed in interlocutory proceedings any party may request the court to order an early trial.

Part XVI: Miscellaneous (Sections 130-140)

Sections 130 to 140 provide for miscellaneous matters relating to proceedings before the Registrar, general powers of the court, the burden of proof in certain cases and the recognition of agents. **Section 130** provides that any decision from the Registrar can be appealed to the court unless the rules state otherwise. **Section 131** deals with the Registrar's right to be heard or represented in any court proceedings involving the alteration or rectification of the register. **Section 132**

deals with the general powers of the court and the provision for appeal to the Court of Appeal. **Section 133** provides for the procedures where application can be made to the court or the Registrar. **Section 134** provides for the reversal of the burden of proof in the case where the invention for which the patent is granted is a process for obtaining a new product. This is a requirement of the Agreement on Trade Related Aspects of Intellectual Property. **Section 135** provides that on exercise of any discretion given by the *Patents Ordinance* by the Registrar a right to be heard must be given to any party to the proceedings. **Sections 136 and 137** deal with costs in proceedings before the court and the Registrar. **Section 138** deals with licences made by order of the court or the Registrar. **Section 139** provides for the immunity of the Registrar and confirms that no patent granted shall be taken as a warranty by the Registrar that it is valid. **Section 140** provides that any act which has to be done by any person in connection with a patent or with obtaining a patent may be done by a duly authorised agent. No restrictions are imposed on who may be an agent but the Registrar has the right to refuse to recognise an agent who does not reside or have a place of business in Hong Kong.

Part XVII: Offences (Sections 141-145)

Sections 141 to 145 set out the criminal offences in respect of the falsification of the register, an unauthorised claim that a patent has been granted or applied for and misuse of the title 'Patents Registry' and regulate the position where offences are committed by corporations or partners.

Part XVIII: Administrative Provisions (Sections 146-153)

Sections 146 to 153 contain administrative provisions including the right of the Registrar to correct errors or mistakes in accordance with the Rules, the method and manner of providing information about patents and patent applications and inspection of documents and the hours of business and excluded days.

Section 149 confers the power on the Registrar to make rules to regulate the practice and procedure under the *Patents Ordinance*.[6] **Section 150** confers the power on the Registrar to require the use of such forms as may be specified by notice in the Gazette in any proceedings before him.[7]

Sections 151 and 152 state that the provisions of the Ordinance bind the Government and that the Government has the right to sell forfeited articles. **Section 153** gives the Chief Executive-in-Council the power to amend or add to the list of countries, territories or areas which are parties to or members of the Paris Convention or the World Trade Organisation.

Part XIX: Repeals and Transitional Arrangements (Sections 154-163)

Sections 154 to 163 deal with repeals, transitional arrangements and consequential amendments.

Section 154 repeals the *Registration of Patents Ordinance*. **Sections 155 to 157** provide for the transitional arrangements in respect of the validity of instruments, and other things made under the repealed Ordinance, the use of patented inventions for service of the Crown and infringement. **Section 158** contains the provisions which allow the Chief Executive-in-Council to make Rules providing for the application of the Ordinance and the continued application of the repealed *Registration of Patents Ordinance* to certain categories of patents and applications for patents.[8] **Section 159** contains the definition of terms for the purposes of ss 154-159.

Sections 160-163 contain the consequential amendments to other Ordinances

Schedule 1

Schedule I sets out those countries which have acceded to the Paris Convention and those countries, territories or areas which are members of the World Trade Organisation.

Schedule 2

Schedule 2 sets out the provisions of section 7G of the repealed *Registration of Patents Ordinance*.

Notes

1 Sections 36 and 54 *Patents (General Rules).*

2 Patents (Designation of Patent Offices) Notice.

3 Sections 36 and 54 *Patents (General) Rules.*

4 Sections 56-57 *Patents (General) Rules.*

5 Section 73 and Schedule 1 *Patents (General) Rules.*

6 *Patents (General) Rules.*

7 Notice of Specification of Forms.

8 *Patents (Transitional Arrangements) Rules.*

8 The Patents (General) Rules Explained

As explained in Chapter 3 the *Patents (General) Rules* are divided into Parts I to XV and three Schedules and deals with the procedures laid down in the *Patents Ordinance* and other specific matters. The *Patents (General) Rules* also deal with certain specific matters as required by the *Patents Ordinance* including specifying the Searching Authorities from whom a search report for the purposes of filing a short-term patent will be accepted, detailing the opposition and post grant rectification proceedings in the designated patent offices which apply for the purposes of ss 43, 44 and 91 of the *Patents Ordinance*, specifying the type of exhibition or meeting which applies for s 95(b) of the *Patents Ordinance,* and specifying the dates of publication or other relevant date as indicates the date of entry into the designated patent office or the Chinese Patent Office in the case of an international application.

The Patents (General) Rules	
Part I	Preliminary
Part II	Applications for Standard Patents
Part III	Provisions as to Applications for Standard Patents before Grant
Part IV	Provisions as to Patents after Grant
Part V	Property in Patents and Applications; Registration
Part VI	Employees' Inventions
Part VII	Revocation of Patents
Part VIII	Language of Proceedings; Authentic Text
Part IX	Applications for Short-term Patents
Part X	Procedures Up To and Including Grant of Short-term Patent
Part XI	Provisions as to Short-term Patents after Grant
Part XII	Hearings and Agents
Part XIII	Information and Inspection

The Patents (General) Rules	
Part XIV	Miscellaneous
Part XV	Transitional
Schedule 1	Micro-Organisms
Schedule 2	Fees
Schedule 3	Modified Application of the Patents (General) Rules to Applications for Standard Patents by Virtue of the Patents (Transitional Arrangements) Rules

Part I: Preliminary (Sections 1 & 2)

Section 1 provides that the Rules will come into operation on the same day as the *Patents Ordinance*.

Section 2 sets out the interpretation provisions for the Rules. Some of the main definitions are set out below:

- The term *application number* in relation to a designated patent application or designated patent refers to the number given by the designated patent office for that purpose and in relation to an application for a standard patent or a short-term patent refers to the number given to it by the Registrar
- The term *Chinese Patent Office*, *European Patent Office* and *United Kingdom Patent Office* refers to offices established under the laws of the respective jurisdictions for granting patents.
- The term *International Patent Classification* refers to the classification system established by the Strasbourg Agreement 1971.
- The term *publication number* in relation to a document published under the *Patents Ordinance* is the number given by the Registrar; in relation to a document published under any other patent laws or an international convention, it is the number given by the relevant patent office; and in the case of the PCT, the number given by the International Bureau.
- The meaning of the term *filing* or *being filed* includes sending, giving, leaving, making or furnishing.
- References in the Rules to a document being in a *specified form* means a document being in a form specified by the Registrar under s 150 of the *Patents Ordinance* and published in the Hong Kong Government Gazette.

Part II: Applications for Standard Patents (Sections 3-26)

This Part deals with the application procedures for a standard patent.

Sections 3 and 4 set out the procedures for making a reference to the Registrar on who has a right to apply for a standard patent including the provisions for opposing such an application and for the making of orders following on from such a reference. **Sections 5-7** sets the procedures for giving notice to interested parties where an order is made and for reference to the Registrar in relation to a licence.

Sections 8-18 set out the requirements for filing a request to record and **Sections 19-26** set out the requirements for making the request for registration and grant.

Sections 8 and 19 set out the specific requirements and content of the request to record a designated patent application and the request for registration and grant of a designated patent and the documents to be filed in support. **Sections 9 and 20** set out the requirements for the documents which are to be filed in support of a statement showing the applicant's right to apply on filing the request to record or request for registration and grant. **Section 10** sets out the details required relating to a previous disclosure at an international exhibition.

Sections 11 and 21 contain the provisions allowing for the period of grace in which to pay the filing or advertisement fee on filing the request to record and the request for registration and grant. **Sections 12 and 13** set out the requirements for the size and presentation of documents and the form of statements, counter-statements and evidence. **Sections 14 and 22** require the Registrar to issue a receipt on first receiving any of the documents comprising the request to record or the request for registration and grant.

Section 15 provides for the date of publication of the designated patent application for the purpose of filing an application which is based on an international application as required by s 16 *Patents Ordinance*.

Sections 16-17 and 23-26 set out the provisions for making good any deficiencies in the documents making up the request to record and the request for registration and grant of the standard patent , including making an application for restoration of rights.

Section 18 sets out the detail of making a request to record a divisional application for a standard patent.

Part III: Provisions as to Applications for Standard Patents before Grant (Sections 27-31)

Section 27 sets out the requirements for filing an application to amend a standard patent application. **Sections 28 and 29** set out the requirements for maintaining an application for a standard patent and the procedures for making good deficiencies in any such application for maintenance. **Sections 30 and 31** deal with the notification by the Registrar that a standard patent has been deemed withdrawn and the procedures for making an application for restoration of an application for a standard patent which has not been maintained.

Part IV: Provisions as to Patents after Grant (Sections 32-41)

This Part sets out the procedures dealing with certain aspects of the standard and short-term patent after grant. **Sections 32-34** set out the procedures for renewal of standard patents, the notification by the Registrar that a standard patent has lapsed and application for restoration of lapsed standard patents.

Section 35 sets out the procedures for amendment of a standard patent under s 43 of the *Patents Ordinance* and sets the prescribed period of three months for filing an amendment. **Section 36** prescribes the opposition or revocation proceedings in the Chinese Patent Office under Articles 41-44 of the Chinese Patent Law and the European Patent Office under Part V of the European Patent Convention for the purposes of ss 43 and 44 of the *Patents Ordinance*. **Section 37** sets the procedures for filing an application for revocation of a standard patent with the Registrar under s 44 of the *Patents Ordinance* and for opposition to such application.

Section 38 sets out the procedures for an inventor to apply to the Registrar for a finding that he is entitled to be mentioned in the patent as the inventor under s 46 of the *Patents Ordinance* and for an opposition to such application .

Section 39 sets out requirements for filing with the Registrar the relevant particulars when the specification of a patent has been amended by court order under s 46 of the *Patents Ordinance*. **Section 40** sets out the procedures on surrender of a patent by the proprietor.

Section 41 sets the procedures for making a reference to the Registrar to revoke a patent on grounds of *ordre public* or morality and for the proprietor to contest the reference.

Part V: Property in Patents and Applications; Registration (Sections 42-52)

Section 42 sets out the requirement to have an address for service in Hong Kong and the procedures for recording such address. **Section 43** sets out the entries to be made in the register upon publication of an application for a standard patent or on grant of the short-term patent and provides that no entry shall be made until such publication or grant. **Section 44** provides for an entry in the register on an application before grant of a standard patent as to who has the right to apply.

Section 45 sets out the procedures for recording in the register an alteration of the name or address or of an address for service of any person entered in the register including the applicant or proprietor or his agent. **Section 46** sets the procedures for an application to register or give notice to the Registrar of any transactions, instruments or events affecting rights in patents or applications for standard patents.

Section 47 sets out the procedures for making a request for correction of errors in the register or in any document filed in connection with the registration. **Section 48** sets the procedures for applying for correction of an error of translation or transcription or of a clerical error or mistake in patents and applications for patents including an error in the specification or document filed in support of an application under s 46 of the *Patents Ordinance* and for any opposition to such application.

Sections 49-51 set the procedures for inspecting the register and obtaining certificates and copies of the entries on the register. **Section 52** sets out the requirements for filing orders or directions given by the court in relation to a patent or application

Part VI: Employees' Inventions (Section 53)

Section 53 sets the prescribed time period in which an application for compensation can be made to the court by an employee.

Part VII: Revocation of Patents (Sections 54-55)

Section 54 prescribes the opposition or revocation proceedings in the Chinese Patent Office under Articles 41-44 of the Chinese Patent Law and the European Patent Office under Part V of the Paris Convention for the purposes of revocation of a standard patent under s 91(1)(i) of the *Patents Ordinance*. **Section 55** prescribes the exhibition or meetings at which disclosure of an invention which is the subject of a standard patent application will be considered as being a non-prejudicial disclosure for the purposes of s 95(1)(b) of the *Patents Ordinance,* namely, an official international exhibition within the terms of the Convention on International Exhibitions or an international exhibition sponsored or recognised by the Chinese Government or academic or technological meetings recognised by the Chinese Government.

Part VIII: Language of the Proceedings (Sections 56-57)

Section 56 sets out the requirements for filing translations of documents or parts of those documents which are not in one of the official languages, the information to be supplied in both official languages, the language to be used in oral proceedings and for a change to the language of the proceedings. **Section 57** sets out the requirements for filing a corrected translation of the specification where the translation confers a narrower protection under s 106(3) of the *Patents Ordinance*.

Part IX: Short-term Patents (Sections 58-74)

Sections 58-74 set out the procedures and requirements for making an application for a short-term patent.

Section 58 sets out the requirements for the application for a short-term patent. **Section 59, 60, 61 and 64** set out the content and requirements for the description, drawings, abstract and claims. **Sections 62 and 63** set out the requirements for the size and presentation of documents and the form of statements, counter-statements and evidence. **Section 65** sets out the statements and procedures where the applicant is not the inventor and for notice to be given to the inventor or inventors .

Section 66 provides for the issue of receipt by the Registrar on first receipt of any documents comprising an application for a short-term patent. **Sections 67 and 68** set out the provisions and time periods for making good any deficiencies in the documents making up the short-term patent application and for the grace period for payment of the filing and advertising fees.

Section 69 sets out the procedures for claiming priority of a short-term patent under the Paris Convention. **Section 70** sets out the requirements and details to be given on making a claim regarding a non-prejudicial disclosure.

Section 71 prescribes the Searching Authorities for the purposes of obtaining a Search report under s 113(8) of the *Patents Ordinance*, namely, the International Searching Authorities appointed under Article 16 of the PCT and the designated patent offices. **Section 72** sets out the requirements for the search report and its content.

Section 73 and **Schedule 1** set out the requirements concerning applications for short-term patents which require for their performance the use of micro-organisms.

Section 74 set out the requirements for making a divisional short-term patent application.

Part X: Procedure Up To and Including Grant of Short-term Patents (Sections 75-78)

Section 75 sets out the procedures for making an application to amend a short-term patent application. **Sections 76 and 77** set out the requirement for giving notice requesting reinstatement and an application for restoration of rights of an application for a short-term patent.

Section 78 provides for the date of issuance of the National Application Notification by the Chinese Patent Office to be the alternative date under s 125 *Patents Ordinance* for the purposes of a short-term patent application based on an international application.

Part XI: Provisions as to Short-term Patents after Grant (Sections 79-81)

Section 79 sets out the procedures for renewal of short-term patents. **Section 80** sets out the requirement by the Registrar to give notification of a lapsed short-term patent. **Section 81** provides that the procedures for restoration of lapsed short-term patents as set in s 34 of the Rules applies to short-term patents .

Part XII: Hearings and Agents (Section 82-87)

Section 82 sets out the procedures for a request for hearing of a person adversely affected by the exercise of a discretion by the Registrar and for the issue of a decision by the Registrar. **Section 83** provides that a hearing will be held in public unless the Registrar directs otherwise. **Section 84** sets out the requirements where a document is to be signed by partnerships, companies and associations. **Section 85** sets out the requirements when acts are done by an agent and the requirement for evidence of authority of such an agent in certain circumstances. **Sections 86 and 87** contain matters relating to the award of costs and the giving of security for costs

Part XIII: Information and Inspection (Sections 88-92)

Section 88 sets out the cases where information relating to a standard patent or standard patent application can be made under s 147. **Section 89** sets out the restrictions on the documents which can be inspected. **Section 90** sets out the procedures and requirements in relation to confidential documents. **Section 91** sets out the specific bibliographic information which can be published or made available in relation to a short-term patent application and an unpublished standard patent application under s 147(3) of the *Patents Ordinance*. **Section 92** sets out the procedures for making available information in relation to a short-term patent application and an unpublished standard patent application in the circumstances outlined in s 147(4) of the *Patents Ordinance*.

Part XIV: Miscellaneous (Sections 93-104)

Section 93 sets out the requirements in relation to the service of documents. **Sections 94 and 95** allow the Registrar to amend any document and rectify any irregularity in procedure in or before the Registry on such terms as he may direct. **Section 95** gives the Registrar the power to dispense with certain requirements in certain cases on such terms as he may direct.

Sections 96 and 97 set out the requirements for giving evidence and the making of statutory declarations and affidavits. **Section 98** gives the Registrar power to give directions at any stage of any proceedings before the Registrar. **Section 99** gives the Registrar power to appoint advisers to assist him in any proceedings before the Registrar.

Section 100 provides that the time periods for doing any act and taking any action under the Rules can be extended by the Registrar on request and provides that such extension may be granted even if the time period has expired. This section also specifies those time periods which cannot be extended.

Section 101 allows the Registrar to arrange for publication and sale of copies of the specifications and other documents held in the Registry.

Section 102 provides that a verified copy of a document for the purposes of filing with the Registrar shall be considered as verified if it is certified as a true copy by the person to whose custody the original is committed.

Section 103 allows the Registrar to arrange for the publication and advertisement of such things done under the Ordinance or the Rules as he thinks fit.

Section 104 and **Schedule 2** provide for the list of those fees which are to be paid in relation to specified applications and proceedings under the Ordinance.

Part XV: Transitional (Sections 105 -112)

Sections 105-112 set out certain matters relating to the transitional provisions.

Section 105 provides that terms used in the *Patents (Transitional Arrangements) Rules* have the same meaning when used in the *Patents (General) Rules*. **Section 106** sets out the details to be entered in the register in relation to standard patents granted or deemed to be granted under the *Patents (Transitional Arrangements) Rules*.

Section 107 sets out the procedures for giving notice to the proprietor and for the proprietor to be heard on any deletion from the register of the particulars of a deemed standard patent by the Registrar under s 13(3) of the *Patents (Transitional Arrangements) Rules*. **Section 108** sets out the procedures for making an application to the Registrar to delete from the register any details in relation to a deemed standard patent and for an opposition to such application. **Section 109** sets the procedures for an application under s 13(8) of the *Patents (Transitional Arrangements) Rules*.

Section 110 deals with a request for information relating to patents granted under the *Registration of Patents Ordinance*.

Sections 111-112 and Parts I-II of Schedule 3 provide for the modification of the *Patents (General) Rules* in relation to applications for a standard patent under ss 6, 8, 9 and 7 of the *Patents (Transitional Arrangements) Rules*.

Schedule 1: Micro-Organisms

This Schedule sets out the procedures and requirements when an invention which is the subject of an application for a short-term patent or a short-term patent requires for its performance the use of a micro-organism. Paragraph 1 sets out the requirements on application . Paragraph 2 sets out the provisions in relation to making the cultures available on request being made to the Registrar. Paragraph 3 deals with the position when a new deposit of a culture is required. Paragraph 4 defines the meaning of the term *Budapest Treaty* as being the Treaty on the International Recognition of the Deposit of Micro-Organisms for the purposes of the Patent Procedures done at Budapest in 1977, *international depository authority* as being a depository institution which has acquired that status under the Budapest Treaty and *depository institution* as an institution which carries out the functions of receiving , storing, etc micro-organisms.

Schedule 2: Fees

This Schedule sets out the list of fees which are payable for the specified matters and proceedings under the *Patents Ordinance*.

Schedule 3: Modified Application of the Patents (General) Rules to Applications for Standard Patents by Virtue of the Transitional Rules

Parts I and II of this Schedule set out those parts of the *Patents (General) Rules* which are modified in relation to making applications for a standard patent under the *Patents (Transitional Arrangements) Rules*.

9 Application Procedures for a Standard Patent

The new law provides for the grant of a standard patent based on the registration of patents granted by a designated patent office. The old law provides for registration of patents granted by the United Kingdom Patent Office including European patents (UK) which take effect in the United Kingdom. Both the new law and the old law provide for a registration system but the new law, although in general taking an evolutionary approach, does differ in some areas from the old law.

The application procedures under the new law reflect the differences between the new law and the former system. Thus, for example, under both the old law and the new law, application is made initially to another patent office before application is made in Hong Kong.[1] Apart from this fundamental point the application procedures are new and although there are some similarities they have to be treated as such.

The most important fact to keep in mind is that the time for applying for patent protection in Hong Kong is different. Thus under the new law, application must be made within six months of the publication of the application by the designated patent office in contrast with the old law where application must be made within five years after grant of the patent.

Under the new law, application for a patent will initially be made to the designated patent office. Application will be made in Hong Kong to the Patents Registry for a standard patent in a two-stage procedure in Hong Kong. The application for the standard patent in Hong Kong is made to the Hong Kong Patents Registry at the first stage within six months of the publication of the application by the designated patent office, and at the second stage within six months of the grant of the patent by the designated patent office. Both stages of the application procedure must be complied with to obtain a standard patent.[2]

Application may be made by the applicant or his agent.

Proposed New Law

The relevant provisions relating to the application for a standard patent are contained in Parts II and III of the *Patents Ordinance*. Part II deals with the application procedures for obtaining a standard patent and Part III deals with certain aspects of the application before grant. Part I which covers the definition is also relevant in considering the application requirements. These provisions are outlined in Chapter 7. Much of the detail of the procedures is contained in the *Patents (General) Rules* made by the Registrar under s 148. The forms currently to be used have been specified and published in the Gazette on 27 June 1997.[3]

Meaning of Terms Used and Other Aspects

It is necessary to consider some of the terms used and some other general points before moving on to outline the actual application procedures. Part I of the *Patents Ordinance* contains the main definitions of the terms used in Parts II and III. Those that are of particular relevance are highlighted below.

Patent and standard patent

The term *patent* has been defined to include both a standard patent and a short-term patent. A *standard patent* has been defined as a patent granted under Part II.[4]

Application for a standard patent

Section 3 of the *Patents Ordinance* deals with the meaning of the term *an application for a standard patent*. The term refers to the application from the date of filing the request to record up to grant. This expression does not refer to the standard patent once granted.

Because of the two-stage application procedure in Hong Kong which follows on from original application in and subsequent grant by the designated patent office it is necessary to further clarify the meaning of this term. Accordingly, this Section also makes it clear that references to

- an *application for a standard patent* is a reference to the filing of the request to record;
- *date of filing an application for standard patent* is reference to the date of filing of the request to record; and
- *publication of a standard patent* is a reference to publication of the request to record.

Subject matter of the invention

The new law is a registration system which is based on a patent granted by a designated patent office. It is important to emphasise that the invention which is the subject matter of the standard patent or the application for the standard patent is in fact the invention which is the subject matter of the corresponding designated patent application or designated patent

The *Patents Ordinance* therefore makes it clear that any reference to the *specification of the application for a standard patent* is a reference to the specification of the corresponding designated patent application and that the patent is granted for the invention shown in the published specification of the designated patent as filed with the Registrar.[5]

Request to record and request for registration and grant

The two terms *request to record* and *request for registration and grant* reflect the two-stage application procedure. The term *request to record* refers to the first stage of the application procedure namely the request under s 15 of the *Patents Ordinance* to record a designated patent application. The term *request for registration and grant* refers to the second stage of the application procedure namely the request under s 23 of the *Patents Ordinance* for the registration of the designated patent and the grant of the standard patent .

Date of filing

The term *date of filing* has different meanings depending on the document referred to. The date of filing a request to record and the date of filing an application for a standard patent is in fact the same, ie the date of filing given to the request to record by the Registrar under s 17 of the *Patents Ordinance* after compliance with all the formality requirements. However, the term *date of filing* when used in reference to the designated patent application is the date of filing specified in the designated patent application. This date corresponds with the *deemed date of filing* of the standard patent when granted. The date of filing the request for registration and grant is the date given by the Registrar under s 24 of the *Patents Ordinance* after all the formality requirements have been complied with.

Designated patent application and other aspects.

The terms *designated patent application*, *designated patent* and *corresponding designated patent application* or *designated patent* are all defined in s 4 of Part I of the *Patents Ordinance*.

The term *designated patent application* means the application which has been made to and published by the designated patent office. It includes both the domestic application made directly to and published by the designated patent office and the published international application made via the PCT route which has validly entered the national phase in the designated patent office.

The *designated patent* means the patent granted by the designated patent office. A *corresponding designated patent application* or *designated patent* means the designated patent application or designated patent on which the application in Hong Kong is based.

Published

The meaning of the term *published* has been defined in s 5 of the *Patents Ordinance*. The meaning depends on the context but the term published under the *Patents Ordinance* for the purposes of the application procedures under Part II and III means any document which can be inspected as of right in Hong Kong.

The meaning of the term *published* in relation to publication of the designated patent application by the designated patent office depends on whether it is a domestic application made directly to the designated patent office or an international application made through the PCT route.

If the designated patent application is a domestic application made directly to and published by the designated patent office then *published* means publication by the designated patent office according to the patent law of that office.

If the designated patent application is an international application then *published* means publication of the international application by the World Intellectual Property Organisation unless it is published earlier by the designated patent office.

The term *published* in relation to a designated patent means its publication by the designated patent office according to the patent law of that office.

Designated patent office

A designated patent office is a patent office which has been designated by the Chief Executive-in-Council under s 8 of the *Patents Ordinance* for the purposes of the new law. These offices are the Chinese Patent Office, the European Patent Office for patents designating the United Kingdom and the United Kingdom Patent Office.

Fees on filing a document

The new law confirms a general principle of registration procedures namely that filing a document will only be considered as completed when the fee is paid.[6] The main exception to this rule is that on filing the request to record and request for registration and grant , a date of filing can be accorded without payment of the fee. However, if the fee is not paid within the specified time period the application will be considered as deemed withdrawn.[7]

Formality examination

The new law makes it clear that the Registrar is only required to carry out an examination to ensure that the application complies with the formal requirements and is not required to carry out any substantive search or examination. This is specifically provided in s 11 of the *Patents Ordinance*.

Agents

Any act or procedure which under the *Patents Ordinance* can be done by any person may be done by a duly authorised agent of such person. Such authorisation may be in writing or given orally.[8]

The *Patents (General) Rules* sets out the specific requirements.[9] There is no requirement to file evidence of such authorisation except where the Registrar has some doubts as to the authority of the agent to act. The Registrar may request such evidence where, during any procedures or proceedings before the Registrar, there is a first appointment of an agent or where there is a change in the agent. In such circumstances, the new agent will be required to notify the Registrar on the prescribed form.[10] This reflects the old law and practice in Hong Kong in respect of both trademark and patent registration.

The Patents Steering Committee recommended the maintenance of a register of persons entitled to act as an agent in any procedures or proceedings before the Registrar, but this recommendation was not adopted. The *Patents Ordinance*[11] provides that the Patent Rules may authorise the Registrar to refuse to recognise as an agent any person specified for the purpose in the rules. Section 85(5) of the *Patents (General) Rules* gives the power to the Registrar to refuse to recognise as an agent a person who has a criminal record or has been struck off the roll of solicitors or barristers kept under the *Legal Practitioners Ordinance* (Chapter 159) or who has been suspended from acting as solicitor or barrister.

Amendment of application for standard patent[12]

An application for a standard patent may be amended and details of changes on the register recorded. Special provisions apply to an amendment of the title of the invention, the abstract, a priority claim or any claim description or drawing. Amendment to these particulars can only be made if the standard patent application has been published and if there has been a corresponding amendment to the corresponding designated patent application. An applicant will be required to file verified copies of the amendment in the designated patent office.[13]

Withdrawal of application

An applicant for standard patent may withdraw his application at any time. Such withdrawal cannot be revoked. No withdrawal, amendment of an application or filing of a request to record a divisional designated patent application can be made after the date on which preparations for the publication of the standard patent have been completed.[14]

Registrar may refuse to record or register and grant

The Registrar may refuse to record a designated patent application or register a designated patent and grant standard patent if he considers the invention which is the subject of the application for the standard patent is not a patentable invention because the working of the invention would be contrary to *ordre public* or morality. Such working shall not be deemed to be contrary to *ordre public* or morality merely because is prohibited by or contrary to any law in force in Hong Kong.[15]

Right to Apply for a Standard Patent

The new law differentiates between persons who may apply for the patent and persons who may in fact be entitled to obtain the patent in Hong Kong. This follows the method used in the 1977 Act but takes a different approach. The new law is a registration system which requires the registration of a designated patent application and a designated patent before the standard patent can be granted. For this reason the new law requires a link between the applicant in the designated patent office and the applicant in Hong Kong.

The *Patents Ordinance*[16] accordingly provides that the person who may apply for a standard patent must be

- the applicant for the patent in the designated patent office or his successor in title; or
- any person who may be entitled to the patent in Hong Kong in preference to the designated patent office applicant.

In practical terms the applicant is in most cases likely to be the person named in the designated patent application as the proprietor or his successor in title. If the rights to the invention in Hong Kong are assigned to another person then this successor in title could apply for the standard patent. Alternatively, if for example, the inventor wished to retain the rights to the invention in Hong Kong but not in the designated patent office he could also apply.

Any person having rights to the invention in Hong Kong but who is not the person named as proprietor in the designated patent application would need to show the link between himself and such proprietor when making the application. Provided evidence of such link is filed, the applicant for the standard patent will be taken to be the applicant in any proceedings before the Registrar, unless application is made to the Registrar or the court to determine the question of who has the right to apply.

It is possible for the question of who may apply in Hong Kong for a standard patent to be considered and determined before the grant of the patent. Thus, even before the standard patent is granted any person may make an application to the court or the Registrar to determine any questions as to who may apply for the grant of a standard patent.[17]

The procedures for such an application are[18] laid down in the Patent Rules and the High Court Rules but on making such an application, notice must be given to the applicant for the standard patent and any other person who is alleged to have a right to be granted the patent. Any such person may oppose the application.

This is one of the few instances in the new law where questions can be determined by either the Registrar or the court. In this instance the question to be determined would, in the main, involve contractual questions and not matters relating to the patentability of the invention. The Registrar has the power to refer any such application to the court if he considers it appropriate to do so.

The Registrar or the court may make such order as is thought fit. In particular, an order may be made that the application is to proceed in the name of the applicant in preference to the original applicant or to two applicants jointly. The Registrar or the court also has the power to transfer or grant a licence and to give directions to enable the provisions of the order to be carried out. There are provisions to protect the rights of licensees in the event of any order being made.[19]

It is important to note that any such application will not prevent the grant of the patent once the formality requirements have been satisfied. Thus even if the question has not been determined the patent will be granted. The application will continue to be considered as if it had been considered on an application made after grant.[20] Although applications made after grant can only be made to the court the Registrar will still have power to consider the question referred to him before grant but can only exercise the powers as set out in s 13 of the *Patents Ordinance* and not the greater powers available to the court under s 55 of the *Patents Ordinance*.

Application for a Standard Patent

Application for a standard patent under the new law can be made based on applications for patents which have been published by a patent office after the date on which that office is designated as a designated patent office for the purposes of the new law.

Application for a standard patent has four distinct phases:

Phase 1 begins with the application for a patent in the designated patent office and continues up to the publication of that application by the designated patent office 18 months after the date of application. In the case of an international application the first phase begins with the filing of an application for a patent with a Receiving Office under the PCT and continues until it validly enters the national phase in the designated patent office.

Phase 2 represents the first stage in Hong Kong and begins with the publication of the designated patent application by the designated patent office or valid entry into the national phase of an international application and ends initially when the request to record is recorded and published or the request to record is deemed withdrawn. Application to the Hong Kong Patents Registry for a request to record the designated patent application must be made within six months after the publication of the designated patent application by the designated patent office or the date set in the *Patents (General) Rules* in the case of an international application.[21] The Registrar conducts a formality check and on compliance with the formality requirements the request to record is recorded and published. If the formality requirements are not complied with the application for the standard patent will be deemed withdrawn. Phase 2 takes place in parallel with phase 3 and will finally end when the request for registration and grant is filed. An applicant must maintain the application if the request for registration and grant is not filed and the designated patent application is still pending in the fifth year after the publication of the request to record.

Phase 3 represents the continued processing of the application in the designated patent office. This phase begins after the publication of the designated patent application by the designated patent office and continues until the patent is granted by that office or the application is refused or deemed withdrawn. It does not include the opposition or post grant revocation proceedings in the designated patent office. If the designated patent application is refused or deemed withdrawn the application in Hong Kong cannot proceed.

Phase 4 represents the second stage in Hong Kong and begins after the grant of the designated patent by the designated patent office and ends with the grant and publication of the standard patent or when the request for registration and grant is refused or deemed withdrawn. Application to the Hong Kong Patents Registry for request for registration and grant of the designated patent must be made within six months after the grant of the designated patent by the designated patent office. The Registrar conducts a formality check and on compliance with the formality requirements the designated patent is registered and the standard patent granted and published. If the formality requirements are not complied with the application for the standard patent will be deemed withdrawn.

The procedures in the designated patent office are not the subject of this book and they will be referred to only if they have an impact on the procedures in Hong Kong.

Application in the First Stage in Hong Kong – Filing a Request to Record a Designated Patent Application

The first stage of the application procedure in Hong Kong must be commenced within six months after

- the date of publication of the designated patent application by the designated patent office, in the case of a domestic application made directly to the designated patent office;[22] or
- the date of publication by the designated patent office as serves to indicate that the international application has validly entered the national phase in that designated patent office, in the case of an international application or such other date as prescribed in the rules.[23]

The time will run from the day after the publication of the designated patent application. Each of the proposed designated patent offices have their own procedures for publication of both a domestic application and evidence that an international application has entered the national phase in the relevant designated patent office. It will be necessary to ensure that the date of publication is known so that application can be made in Hong Kong in due time. The relevant dates for the purposes of filing an international application are set out in the *Patents (General) Rules*.

The formal filing requirements for making an application are set out in ss 15 and 16 of the *Patents Ordinance* and ss 8 to 15 *Patents (General) Rules*.[24]

Section 15 of the *Patents Ordinance* sets out the requirements for filing the request to record when the application is based on a domestic application made directly to the designated patent office. Section 16 of the *Patents Ordinance* and s 15 *Patents (General) Rules* provide some modification of s 15 of the *Patents Ordinance* where the designated patent application is based on an international application made under the PCT.

An application for a standard patent may be made by a person entitled to apply under s 12 of the *Patents Ordinance* by requesting the Registrar to enter a record of the designated patent application in the register. The application may be made by the applicant or his agent.

The documents to be filed in making the request to record and the information to be given in support which will together constitute the formal requirements for making an application will be

- an application form;
- certain documents in support; and
- a filing fee and advertisement fee.

Application may be made in either English or Chinese.

An application form[25] will have to be filed. This form has been specified by the Registrar under s 150 of the *Patents Ordinance* in the Notice of Specification of Forms.[26] The form is available in English or Chinese. The form must be completed in the language the applicant wishes to use as the language of the proceedings and thus the language which is used on the form will be the language of the proceedings. The form must be signed by the applicant or his agent.

The following information must be given on the form:

- The reference of the applicant's agent.
- The name and address of the applicant which may be given in English or Chinese but if the name is given in Chinese characters a transliteration of the name must also be given in the roman alphabet.
- A statement indicating whether the applicant is the person named in the designated patent application and if not, confirmation that the supporting documentation is filed.

- The title of the invention as shown in the designated patent application or the international application in both English and Chinese.
- Specified details of the designated patent application, ie
  - (i) the application number allocated to the designated patent application by the designated patent office;
  - (ii) the date of filing in the designated patent office;
  - (iii) the publication number allocated to the designated patent application by the designated patent office; and
  - (iv) the date of publication of the designated patent application.
- If the request is for a designated patent application based on an international application the following information is required:
  - (i) international application number given by the International Bureau of the World Intellectual Property Organisation;
  - (ii) the filing date of the international application;
  - (iii) the publication number of the international application allocated by the International Bureau of the World Intellectual Property Organisation; and
  - (iv) the date of publication in the designated patent office indicating that the international application has validly entered the national phase or the date of issuance of the National Application Notification by the Chinese Patent Office.
- If the application is divided or is derived from an earlier Hong Kong application then the relevant Section of the *Patents Ordinance* under which application is made must be stated[27] together with the following information:
  - (i) the earlier application number in Hong Kong;
  - (ii) the date of filing of the earlier application in Hong Kong; and
  - (iii) the date of publication of the earlier application in Hong Kong.
- If the benefit of the right of priority accorded in the designated patent office is to be claimed under s 98 of the *Patents Ordinance*,[28] then the form must state this and give:
  - (i) the country in which priority is claimed
  - (ii) the application number of the prior application on which the application for priority is claimed;
  - (iii) the date of filing of such prior application; and

(iv) in the case of an international application whether the priority was claimed before the designated patent office or in the international application.

- If the inventor is not named in the designated patent application, the name of the inventor.[29] If the inventor is named in the designated patent application this information is not required. However, if the name of the inventor is only given in Chinese characters a transliteration of the name must also be given in the roman alphabet.
- If a claim is made in the designated patent application in respect of any non-prejudicial disclosure and it is wished to claim the benefit in Hong Kong then the form must state this and give the following information in respect of the claim:[30]
  (i) the name and place of the exhibition;
  (ii) the opening date of such exhibition; and
  (iii) the date of the first disclosure of the invention.
- The form must state the number of sheets for the documents in support. This is an administrative requirement.
- The name and address of the applicant's agent, if any, and an address for service in Hong Kong if the applicant does not have an address in Hong Kong.
- A request to enter a record of the designated patent application in the register.

Documents in support

The following documents are to be filed in support of the application:[31]

- A photocopy, unverified, of the designated patent application as published.[32] It is assumed that a photocopy means a copy which is produced by a photostat to show a direct reproduction of the original rather than a marked up copy of the original. It is interesting to note that one of the core documents is not required to be certified when other documents such as assignments must be verified. In view of this the Registrar should consider moving towards allowing other types of documents to be supplied in photocopy form without verification.
- A duplicate photocopy of the designated patent application as published in loose-leaf form. This is required for computerisation purposes and to allow for the Registrar to provide electronic access to these documents for searching purposes.[33]

- If the applicant is not the current applicant named in the designated patent application, information indicating the derivation of the right of the applicant to apply in Hong Kong. It was the intention of the Patents Steering Committee that in order to simplify filing requirements the applicant would not be required to produce the assignment documentation if an acknowledgement of the applicant's right to apply was given by the applicant for the designated patent application.[34] Thus Clause 4(2)(a) of the model Patents Bill contained in the Patents Steering Committee Report[35] stated that either of the following should be provided, namely:
  - (i) a statement or acknowledgement signed by the applicant named in the designated patent application and the applicant in Hong Kong; or
  - (ii) copies of the documentary evidence in support, for example, assignment of the rights in Hong Kong.

  The provisions as contained in the *Patents Ordinance* and the *Patents (General) Rules*[36] appear to reflect this intention. Thus where the applicant for the standard patent is the successor in title to the person named in the designated patent application then the applicant must produce certified copies of such documents as establish his rights or in the absence of such document a statement confirming the fact of the transfer or assignment. Where the applicant is the inventor then he has to produce such documents as establish his rights. It is assumed that in both cases if the applicant produces a letter of acknowledgement signed by the applicant in the designated patent office this will be accepted by the Registrar without requiring formal assignment or transfer documents.
- The Abstract as contained in the designated patent application as published in both English and Chinese. Thus the applicant will have to supply a translation of the Abstract into the other official language or into both official languages if such abstract is not in the official language.[37] In practical terms this means that if the application for a standard patent is based on a patent application in the United Kingdom Patent Office or the Chinese Patent Office then a translation will be required into the other language. If it is based on a patent application in the European Patent Office which is in German or French then a translation of the Abstract only will be required into English and Chinese.

Filing fee and advertisement fee

The filing fee and the advertisement fee will be set at different amounts. The advertisement fee is intended to cover the costs of advertising the notice of the publication of the request to record in the Hong Kong Government Gazette. The amounts of these fees are set in Schedule 1 to the *Patents (General) Rules*.[38]

There is provision for a grace period for paying the filing and advertisement fee on filing a request to record. Thus if these fees have not been paid within one month after the date of filing the request to record then they may still be validly paid within one month after the Registrar sends notification of the failure to file. This time period cannot be extended and if they are not paid within this time period the application will be considered as withdrawn.

Filing Requirements for an International Application

An international application is an application for a patent made under the PCT. The PCT provides for an international application to be made to a receiving office designating a country which is a member state. The receiving office is the office of one of the member states of the PCT authorised to receive international applications or the International Bureau of the World Intellectual Property Organisation.

All international applications are forwarded to and published by the World Intellectual Property Organisation. In the international phase, an international application is subject to an international search and may at the option of the applicant be subject to an international preliminary examination. Within the time frames set by the PCT an applicant is required to apply to the patent offices of those countries designated in the international application if they wish to obtain a national patent in that country. Once the formality requirements are complied with and the application has validly entered the national phase the application is processed according to the law of the national office.

The grant of a standard patent in Hong Kong is based on the registration of a patent granted by a designated patent office. The first stage of that process in Hong Kong occurs after publication by the designated patent office.

Section 16 of the *Patents Ordinance* therefore adapts s 15 of the *Patents Ordinance* to allow for application in Hong Kong at the first stage within six months after the date of publication of the fact that the international application has validly entered the national phase in the designated patent office. This procedure reflects the nature of the registration system provided under the new law and is similar to the old law where the patent granted or taking effect in the United Kingdom pursuant to the 1977 Act, whether based on a domestic or international application, is registered in Hong Kong after grant.

Thus the first phase in the case of an international application begins with the filing of an application for a patent with a receiving office under the PCT. An applicant for an international application in Hong Kong who wishes to obtain a patent in Hong Kong should designate in his international application any one of the designated patent offices. Such applicant should then follow the procedures of the relevant designated patent office to enter the national phase in that designated patent office. The first phase ends with the publication of the fact of such entry into the national phase. The procedures thereafter follow those for a domestic patent in any of the designated patent offices.

Once that designated patent application validly enters the national phase it is treated as being a designated patent application and can then be used as the basis for the grant of a standard patent in Hong Kong and the normal procedures as adapted by s 16 of the *Patents Ordinance* will apply.

In summary, an international application is applied for and processed in the normal way until it enters the national phase in the designated patent office. Once the international application has entered the national phase in a designated patent office an application must be filed in Hong Kong within six months after the date of the publication in the designated patent office that the national phase has been validly entered to protect the patent in Hong Kong. In the case of Chinese Patent Office where the international application is published by the International Bureau of the World Intellectual Property Organisation in Chinese the application must be filed within six months of the date of issue of National Application Notification.

Diary reminder

No action is required in Hong Kong until the international application enters the national phase in the designated patent office; however, after the date of publication of such entry into the national phase in that office or such other date as specified, a further step has to be taken to obtain protection in Hong Kong.

The date of publication for the purposes of s 15 of the *Patents Ordinance* in respect of an international application is the date of publication in the designated patent office which serves to indicate that the international application has validly entered the national phase in the designated patent office.[39]

The valid entry of the international application into the national phase in all three designated patent offices is a matter of internal record. The date of publication is intended to be the date such entry becomes a matter of public record. Each of the designated patent offices have different procedures for publishing in their official journals the valid entry into the national phase. Such procedures can depend on whether the international application was in the official language of the designated patent office.

In view of this, s 16 (a)(ii) of the *Patents Ordinance* also provides that the date of publication can be such other date as may be prescribed in the Patent Rules provided this date is no earlier than the date of valid entry into the national phase. This gives a degree of flexibility to reflect the different procedures and also allows for changes if any of the designated patent office alter their procedures for such publication.

Section 15 of the *Patents (General) Rules* sets out those dates which are considered to be the date of publication under s 15(2) of the *Patents Ordinance* from which the six months period will run in respect of each designated patent office. These are set out below.

European Patent Office

In the European Patent Office the relevant date is the date of publication by the European Patent Office in the European Patent Office Bulletin of the relevant bibliographic data showing that the international application has entered the domestic phase.

United Kingdom Patent Office

In the United Kingdom the date is the date of publication by the United Kingdom Patent Office in its Official Journal(Patents) of the relevant bibliographic data showing that the international application has entered the domestic phase.

Chinese Patent Office

In the Chinese Patent Office however there are two alternative dates depending on whether the application is published by the International Bureau of the World Intellectual Property Organisation in Chinese or in any other languages.

When the international application is published by the International Bureau in a language other than Chinese, the relevant date is the date of publication by the Chinese Patent Office in its Patent Gazette of the relevant bibliographic data showing that the international application has entered the domestic phase.

However, when the international application is published by the International Bureau in Chinese the relevant date is the date of issue of the National Application Notification by the Chinese Patent Office.

Although the wording of s 15(2)(a) of the *Patents (General) Rules* is not clear it is assumed that the date from which the six months will run is in fact the date of issue of the Notification by the Chinese Patent Office rather than a date six months after the date of such issue.

Filing Requirements as Adapted by s 16

The filing requirements for a request to record a designated patent application which is in the national phase of an international application are essentially the same as that for a domestic designated patent application. Thus, on application the same documents are required as on filing a domestic designated patent application with some adaptation, namely

- an application form;
- certain documents in support; and
- a filing fee and advertisement fee.

Application may be made in either English or Chinese and the same language requirements will apply.

Application Form

The application form specified by the Registrar under s 149 of the *Patents Ordinance* is the same for both an application based on a domestic application and an international application adapted to take account of the different or additional information required.

These differences are highlighted below:

- The details of the international application will have to be given namely:[40]
  - (i) the application number of the international application;
  - (ii) the filing date of the international application;
  - (iii) the publication number and date of publication of the international application by the International Bureau of the World Intellectual Property Organisation; and
  - (iv) the date of publication which serves to indicate entry into the national phase of an international application or, if appropriate, the date of issue by the Chinese Patent Office of the National Application Notification.
- The title of the invention as shown in the international application as published by the International Bureau must be given in both English and Chinese.[41]
- If the benefit of the right of priority accorded in the designated patent office is claimed under s 98 of the *Patents Ordinance* then in addition to the information required in relation to the priority application, the applicant must state[42] whether the claim is based on a right of priority claimed in the designated patent office or in the international application and accepted in the designated patent office.
- The details of the designated patent application will be adapted as appropriate if, for example, there has been no publication by the Chinese Patent Office.

Documents in support

The same documents will be required to be filed in support of the application but with variations to reflect the differences in the supporting documents. The different documents to be filed are highlighted below:[43]

- A photocopy of the international application as published by World Intellectual Property Organisation in lieu of the designated patent application as published;
- A photocopy of any translation of the international application published by the designated patent office;
- A photocopy of any publication of information in the designated patent office concerning the international application;

- A copy of the National Application Notification issued by the Chinese Patent Office, if applicable;[44]
- A duplicate copy of the international application as published by the World Intellectual Property Organisation in loose-leaf form;[45] and
- Translation of the Abstract as contained in the international application or in the designated patent application as published if any into the other official language or into both official languages if such abstract is not in the official language.

Filing fee and advertisement fee

The filing fee and the advertisement fee will be the same as for a request to record based on a domestic application in the designated patent office.

Summary

In summary the differences between an application based on a designated patent application which was an international application relate primarily to the calculation of the date of publication and to the filing of the copy of the international application in lieu of the designated patent application.

Filing Requirements for a Request to Record

The filing requirements are straightforward and consist of filing of the application form, documents in support and the filing and advertisement fees. Much of the content of the application form relates to information contained in the designated patent application.

In practical terms therefore the applicant is required to provide on filing with the Hong Kong Patents Registry the information given to the designated patent office primarily by filing the copy of the published designated patent application together with further information required for a Hong Kong filing. The special factors in filing in Hong Kong are highlighted below.

Name of the inventor

If the inventor is not named in the designated patent application he or she must be named in the application form on filing the request to record. If the name is given in Chinese characters in the designated patent application then a transliteration of the name must also be given in the roman alphabet.

Title of the invention

The title of the invention as set out in the designated patent application will have to be given in the application form in both official languages.

Priority claim

If priority has been claimed and accorded in the designated patent office then the applicant will enjoy the same right of priority in the application in Hong Kong provided that this is claimed on filing the request to record. It is important to claim this on application and to give the relevant information in the application form.

Non-prejudicial disclosure

If a claim for non-prejudicial disclosure was made in the designated patent office the benefit can be taken in Hong Kong provided that the fact of that disclosure and the required data is given on the application form. It is important to claim this on application and to give the relevant information in the application form.

Points to note on documents filed in support

A photocopy of the designated patent application must be filed. As explained below this will not be a minimum requirement to obtain a filing date.

When the applicant in Hong Kong is not the current person named as applicant in the designated patent application further information will be required to show his right to apply in Hong Kong. The information required depends on the nature of the relationship between the applicant in the designated patent office and the applicant in Hong Kong.

However, where this applies the applicant will either have to produce certified copies of relevant documents showing his right to apply or a statement signed by the transferor confirming this fact.[46] If this statement or documentary information is not in English or Chinese it will have to be translated into the language of the proceedings.[47] This is similar to the existing requirements in Hong

Kong but is different from systems based on original application. The need for and the nature of these supporting documents in these circumstances must be borne in mind.

It is to be emphasised that this information is only required if the applicant in Hong Kong differs from the applicant named in the designated patent application. There is no specific requirement on filing to show the link between the inventor and the applicant in Hong Kong.

Abstract

The abstract as shown in the designated patent application must be translated into the other official language or where appropriate into both official languages. This will not be a minimum requirement to obtain a filing date.

Formality Examination by the Registrar

On receipt of the request to record the Registrar will carry out a formality check to see whether the formal requirements have been complied with so that a filing date can be given and the request to record can be recorded and published.

In order to give a filing date the Registrar examines the application to see whether it complies with the minimum requirements.[48] If a filing date is accorded, a further examination is carried out to see whether all the formal requirements have been satisfied. If they have then the Registrar will record the designated patent application and enter the particulars of the request to record in the register and publish the request to record. If the formal requirements have not been satisfied, the Registrar will ask the applicant to make good the deficiencies in a set time. If the deficiencies are made good then the Registrar will record the designated patent application; otherwise the application will be deemed withdrawn.[49] There are provisions which allow for further processing or the restoration of rights in the event of the failure of the applicant to make good the deficiencies within the times set by the Registrar.[50]

These provisions are intended to be user-friendly but are designed to ensure that the request to record is published as soon as possible after the application is made. This is in the interests of both the applicant and users of the system.

Minimum Requirements to Obtain a Filing Date for the Application

A filing date can be given if within six months after the date of publication the applicant or his agent files with the Registrar[51]

- information which indicates that a request to record is made;
- information which identifies the applicant; and
- reference to the designated patent application including:
  - (i) the application number of the designated patent application;
  - (ii) the publication number of the designated patent application; and
  - (iii) the date of publication.

If at least part of this information is filed within the six-month period the Registrar may request that the full details are given within a further one month period. If this information is given within that further period then a filing date will be given.[52] This period cannot be extended.[53]

If the full information required by s 17 of the *Patents Ordinance* is not given before the expiry of the six-month period or within the time allowed by the Registrar under s 18 of the *Patents Ordinance* the application will not be considered as an application. Thus the provisions for further processing and restoration cannot apply.

The payment of the filing and advertisement fees is not a minimum requirement. These fees must, however, be paid within one month of the earliest date of filing the request to record. If the fees are not so paid these fees, and an additional late payment fee, can still be paid during a further grace period of up to one month. This period is a one-month period after the issue by the Registrar of a notification of the failure to pay the fee where such fee can be validly paid.[54]

Thus, if only part of the minimum requirements are filed but the full requirements are filed within the additional time allowed by the Registrar the filing fee must be paid within one month of the first filing or within the grace period. The effect of the grace period is that if the minimum requirements have been complied the filing fee or advertisement fee can be validly paid within one month after notification by the Registrar of the failure to pay the fee and on payment of the filing and advertisement fee together with the additional fee.

The provisions for further processing an application for a standard patent or restoration of rights contained in ss 28 and 29 of the *Patents Ordinance* do not apply to the failure to comply with the filing of the minimum requirements as the request to record will not be considered as an application or the failure to pay the filing fee in the time set or in the further time allowed by the Registrar.[55] Thus although the minimum requirements are user friendly they must be complied with in the times set.

Diary reminder

To obtain a filing date it is important to note that

- the minimum requirements or part of them must be filed within six months after the date of publication of the designated patent application or the date specified in the case of an international application;
- any deficiencies must be made good within the one-month period set by the Registrar;
- the filing fee and advertisement fee must be paid within one month of the first filing of any part of the request to record or within the further grace period on payment of the additional filing fee; and
- the times set by the Registrar cannot be extended and the provisions as to further processing and restoration do not apply.

Formality examination at the first stage

If a filing date has been given and if the filing and advertisement fees have been paid the Registrar will carry out a full formality examination to see whether the requirements of ss 15 and 16 of the *Patents Ordinance* have been complied with.

If there are deficiencies the Registrar will inform the applicant or his agent of these and ask for them to be made good within two months of the date of the notice.[56] This time may be extended for a further period of two months on request and on payment of a fee.[57]

Further periods in which to comply with the requirements may be allowed by the Registrar on request and on payment of a penalty fee where the only deficiency outstanding is the failure to file a translation of the title of the invention, the abstract of the invention or the transliteration of the name of the applicant or the inventor.[58] This does not apply to the filing of translations for other documents required on filing such as translations of the documents in support of the applicant's right to apply.

If there are no deficiencies or if notified deficiencies are made good within the times set the Registrar will proceed to record the designated patent application and the relevant particulars in the register and publish the request to record. If the deficiencies are not made good the application will either be refused or if no action is taken to comply with the requirements the application will be deemed withdrawn.

There are provisions which allow for further processing or restoration of an application which has been refused or is deemed withdrawn. Thus an application may be reinstated if within two months after the application is refused or deemed withdrawn the applicant requests reinstatement in writing, makes good the outstanding requirements and pays the relevant fees. In addition, it is possible in certain circumstances for the application to be restored. An application for restoration can be made up to one year after the application is refused or deemed withdrawn at the discretion of the Registrar on making good the deficiency and payment of the filing fees. The Registrar will only allow such restoration if he considers that the failure to comply with the time limit occurred in spite of the applicant having taken all reasonable care in the circumstances.

In summary, an applicant has two months after the Registrar gives notice of deficiencies in the filing to comply with the requirements. One extension of two months can be requested on payment of filing fees. In essence therefore, an applicant has four months after notification in which to make good the filing requirements. Further time will be allowed to file translations of the abstract and the title of the invention if all other requirements have been filed. No further extensions are allowed but further processing will be allowed if application is filed within two months after the date of refusal or deemed withdrawal.

These time periods are quite tight and rather less generous than originally intended.[59] However, taking account of the nature of the documentation required, it should not present difficulties but patent owners need to be aware of the importance of supplying the relevant information within these time frames.

Publication of the Request to Record

If the formal requirements of the request to record are met the Registrar will[60]

- record the designated patent application in the register;
- enter the particulars of the request to record in the register;
- publish the request to record;
- advertise the fact of publication in the Hong Kong Government Gazette; and
- inform the applicant.

The *Patents Ordinance* makes it clear that for the purposes of publication, the request to record includes the designated patent application as published, the name of the proprietor and if different, the name of the inventor.[61]

On publication the Registrar will make the request to record and the register available for inspection at the Hong Kong Patents Registry.

Even if the formal requirements are met, the Registrar will not publish the application if before completion of preparations for publication the application has been finally refused or withdrawn or has been deemed to have been withdrawn or if the filing or advertisement fee has not been paid.

In addition, the Registrar has a residual power under s 37 of the *Patents Ordinance* to refuse to record a designated patent application if he considers that the invention which is the subject of the application is not a patentable invention because it is contrary to *ordre public* or morality.

Application in the Second Stage in Hong Kong

The second stage of the application procedure in Hong Kong must be commenced within six months after the date of grant of the designated patent by the designated patent office, or within six months after the grant of the designated patent and the publication of the request to record whichever is the later in the case where the designated patent is granted before publication of the request to record.[62]

The time will run from the day after the publication of the designated patent application.

Filing Requirements

The formal filing requirements for making an application are set out in s 23 of the *Patents Ordinance* and s 19 of the *Patents (General) Rules*.

An application can be made by the applicant for the standard patent or his successor in title to request the registration of the designated patent and the grant of a standard patent. Application can only be made if the request to record has been published and has not been refused or deemed withdrawn or abandoned. Application may be made by the applicant or his agent.

Filing requirements for request for registration and grant under s 23 of the Patents Ordinance

The documents to be filed and the information to be given in support which will constitute the formal requirements for making an application for request for registration and grant are

- an application form;
- certain documents in support; and
- a filing fee and advertisement fee.

The application should be made in the same language in which the request to record was made which will be the language of the proceedings.

Application form

An application form[63] will have to be filed. This form has been specified by the Registrar under s 150 of the *Patents Ordinance* in the Notice of Specification of Forms published on 27 June 1997. The information set out below will be required to be given in the application form:

- Reference of the applicant or his agent;
- Details of the corresponding request to record namely
  - (i) the application number;
  - (ii) the publication number ; and
  - (iii) date of publication.
- The name and address of the applicant. If the language of the proceedings is Chinese the name will also have to be given in the roman alphabet;

- If the applicant is not the current applicant recorded in the register a statement indicating the derivation of the right of the applicant to make the request for registration and grant;
- Title of the invention in English and Chinese;
- Specified details of the designated patent application, ie
  - (i) the publication number allocated to the designated patent by the designated patent office; and
  - (ii) the date of grant of the designated patent;
- The number of sheets of the supporting documents;
- Name and address of the agent, if any. Any change in the agent appointed in the request to record will need to be notified and is likely to have to be supported by evidence of such appointment. If the applicant does not have an address in Hong Kong an address for service in Hong Kong; and
- Request to register the designated patent and grant a standard patent.

Documents in support

Certain documents will have to be filed in support of the request to register the designated patent and the grant of the standard patent.

- A verified copy of the designated patent as published will have to be filed.[64] The copy can be verified by the designated patent office or can be verified as a true copy by the person who holds the original.[65]
- A duplicate copy of the designated patent application as published in loose-leaf form will also be required.[66] The copy is required for computerisation purposes and to enable electronic access to the register. Such copy will not need to be verified.
- If the applicant is not the current applicant for the standard patent as recorded in the register, a statement indicating the derivation of the right of the applicant to apply in Hong Kong and such documents in support as show that such person is so entitled. It is assumed that documents similar to that prescribed by s 9 of *Patents (General) Rules* will be accepted by the Registrar.[67]

Filing fee and advertisement fee

The filing fee and the advertisement fee will be set at different amounts. The advertisement fee is intended to cover the costs of advertising the notice of the publication of the request to record in the Hong Kong Government Gazette. The amounts of these fees are set in the Patents Rules Schedule 1.[68]

Comment

The filing requirements are straightforward and consist of the filing of the application form, documents in support and the filing and advertisement fees. Much of the content of the application form relates to information contained in the designated patent.

In practical terms therefore on filing with the Hong Kong Patents Registry the applicant is required to provide the information obtained on the grant of the designated patent primarily by filing the copy of the granted designated patent and also to supply further information required for a Hong Kong filing. The special factors in filing in Hong Kong are highlighted below.

Any changes in the name or address of the applicant for the standard patent, in the name and address of the agent or any change in the address for service not already recorded must be made at this stage.

The *Patents Ordinance* provides that if priority has been claimed and accorded in the designated patent office then the applicant may be required by the Patent Rules to supply copies of the priority documents lodged with the designated patent office. The *Patents (General) Rules* do not currently contain any such requirement

Points to note on documents filed in support

A copy of the designated patent duly verified will be required. As explained below this will not be a minimum requirement to obtain a filing date.

If an applicant for the request for registration and grant is not the person currently named as proprietor in the designated patent or is not the person recorded in the register as the applicant for the standard patent then documents in support of his right to make the request will be required.

This requirement will only arise if there are changes in the proprietor in the designated patent office or in the applicant for the standard patent. There are a number of different circumstances which could arise and the need to file a statement or evidence in support will have to be assessed in the circumstances of each case.

If for example, the applicant for the standard patent and the proprietor in the designated patent office are not the same, supporting information may be required. If they are in fact the same persons as shown as the applicant for the request to record and the applicant named in the designated patent application, respectively, then the documents filed with the request to record may be sufficient to show the right of the applicant to make the request for registration and grant. Another scenario is where the applicant shown in the register and the applicant named in the designated patent application are the same but the designated patent application has subsequently been assigned to the current proprietor of the designated patent. In this case a statement explaining the derivation and documentary evidence to establish who is entitled to make the request for registration and grant will be required.

It has to be emphasised that this information will only be required if the applicant shown on the register and the proprietor of the designated patent are different. If the applicant or proprietor in the designated patent office is the same as the applicant in Hong Kong and any changes to the applicant or proprietor are made in the designated patent office it would seem sensible to also record such changes in the register in Hong Kong. This would simplify the requirements on making the request for registration and grant.

Formality Examination by the Registrar at the Second Stage

The formality requirements at the second stage will mirror those at the first stage. Thus, on receipt of the request for registration and grant the Registrar will carry out a formality check to see whether the formal requirements have been complied with so that a date of filing can be given and the designated patent can be registered and the standard patent granted.

In order to give a date of filing the Registrar will examine the application to see if it complies with the minimum requirements. If a date of filing is accorded, a further examination is carried out to determine if all the formal requirements have been satisfied.[69] If they have then the Registrar will register the designated patent and grant the standard patent. If all the formal requirements have not been met the Registrar will ask the applicant to make good the deficiencies within a set time.[70] If the deficiencies are made good within these times then the Registrar will register the designated patent and grant the standard patent. If the deficiencies are not made good the application will either be refused or if no action is taken be deemed withdrawn. There are provisions which allow for further processing or the restoration of rights in the event of the failure of the applicant to make good the deficiencies within the times set by the Registrar.

Minimum Requirements to Obtain a Filing Date at the Second Stage

A date of filing can be given if, within six months after the date of grant of the patent, or, the date of publication of the request to record if it is later than the grant of the designated patent, the applicant or his agent files with the Registrar

- information which indicates that a request for registration and grant is being made;
- information which identifies the applicant;
- the publication number of the designated patent and date of publication; and
- the publication number of the request to record.

If no part of the information is given before the expiry of the six-month period the application for a standard patent will be deemed withdrawn.

If at least part of this information is filed within the six-month period the Registrar may request that the full details are given within a further one-month period. If this information is given within that further period then a date of filing will be given.[71]

If the full information required by s 24 of the *Patents Ordinance* is not given before the expiry of the six-month period or within the further time allowed by the Registrar under s 24 of the *Patents Ordinance* the application will be deemed withdrawn.[72]

Note that the payment of the filing and advertisement fees is also not a minimum requirement at the filing at the second stage. These fees must however be paid within one month of the earliest date of filing the request to register. If it is not so paid a further grace period of up to one month may be allowed by the Registrar. Thus, if only part of the minimum requirements are filed and the full requirements are filed within the additional time allowed by the Registrar the filing and advertisement fees must still be paid within one month of the first filing or within the further grace period allowed by the Registrar together with the additional filing fee.[73]

The provisions for further processing an application for a standard patent or restoration of rights contained in ss 28 and 29 of the *Patents Ordinance* do not apply to the failure to comply with the filing of the minimum requirements or the failure to pay the filing fee in the time set or in the further time allowed by the Registrar. Thus, although the minimum requirements are user friendly they must be complied with in the times set.

In order to avoid paying additional fees the filing and advertisement fees should be paid on filing some part of the minimum requirements or within one month of that date.

Diary reminder for obtaining a filing date for the request for registration and grant

To obtain a filing date it is important to note that

- the minimum requirements or part of them must be filed before the expiry of the period of six months after the date of grant of the designated patent or if later, the date of publication of the request to record;
- all the minimum requirements must be made good in the times set by the Registrar;
- the filing fee and advertisement fee must be paid within one month of the first filing of any part of the request to record or within the further one month grace period allowed by the Registrar; and
- the times set by the Registrar cannot be extended and the provisions as to further processing and restoration do not apply to these minimum filing requirements.

Formality Examination at the Second Stage

If a filing date has been given and if the filing and advertisement fees have been paid the Registrar will carry out a full formality examination to see whether the requirements of s 23 of the *Patents Ordinance* have been met.

If there are deficiencies the Registrar will inform the applicant or his agent of these and ask for them to be made good within the time periods set in the *Patents (General) Rules*. These periods are the same for both stages. Thus the Registrar may set a time of two months initially with a power to extend this by a further period of two months on request by the applicant and on payment of the relevant fees.[74]

Further periods in which to comply with the requirements may be allowed by the Registrar on request and on payment of a penalty fee where the only deficiency outstanding is the failure to file a translation of the title of the invention or the transliteration of the name of the applicant or the inventor.[75] This does not apply to the filing of translations for other documents required on filing such as translations of the documents in support of the applicant's right to make the request.

If there are no deficiencies or if the notified deficiencies are made good within the times set the Registrar will proceed to register the designated patent and grant the standard patent. If the deficiencies are not made good the application will either be refused or if no action is taken to comply with the requirements the application will be deemed withdrawn.

In addition, the provisions which allow for further processing or restoration apply at the second stage in the same way as at the first stage. Thus an application may be reinstated if within two months after the application is refused or deemed withdrawn the applicant requests reinstatement in writing, makes good the outstanding requirements and pays the relevant fees. It is also possible in certain circumstances for the application to be restored. An application for restoration can be made up to one year after the application is refused or deemed withdrawn at the discretion of the Registrar on making good the deficiency and payment of the filing fees. The Registrar will only allow such restoration if he considers that the failure to comply with the time limit occurred in spite of the applicant having taken all reasonable care in the circumstances.

In summary, these provisions mirror the provisions at the first stage and an applicant has two months after the Registrar gives notice of deficiencies in the filing to comply with the requirements. One extension of two months can be requested on payment of filing fees. In essence therefore, an applicant has four months after notification in which to make good the filing requirements. Further time will be allowed to file translations of the title of the invention and the transliteration of the name of the applicant or the inventor if all other requirements have been filed. No further extensions are allowed but further processing will be allowed if application is filed within two months after the date of refusal or deemed withdrawal.

These time periods are quite tight and rather less generous than originally intended. However, taking account of the nature of the documentation required it should not present difficulties but patent owners need to be aware of the importance of supplying the relevant information within these time frames.

Registration of Designated Patent and Grant of Patent

If the formal requirements of the request to record are met[76] the Registrar will

- register the designated patent by making the appropriate entries in the register;
- grant the standard patent for the invention shown in the published specification of the designated patent as filed;
- issue a certificate of grant;
- publish the specification of the standard patent, the names of the proprietor and the inventor if different; and
- advertise the fact of grant in the Hong Kong Government Gazette and inform the applicant.

On publication the Registrar will make the specification of the standard patent and the register available for inspection by the public at the Hong Kong Patents Registry.

It is important to note that the Registrar has a residual power under s 37 of the *Patents Ordinance* to refuse to register the designated patent and grant the standard patent if he considers that the invention which is the subject of the application is not a patentable invention because it is contrary to *ordre public* or morality.

Divisional Applications

The *Patents Ordinance* contains provisions which allow for a request to record to be made where the designated patent application is divided.[77]

The right to make a request to record in respect of a divisional designated patent application arises only where a request to record has been published in respect of the corresponding designated patent application which is being divided.

In such a case if the corresponding designated patent application is divided, the applicant for the standard patent may within six months of the publication of the divisional designated patent application or publication of the request to record, whichever is the later, request the Registrar to record the divisional designated patent application in the register. The normal provisions of the *Patents Ordinance* in relation to the filing of a request to record and a request for registration and grant apply to such request to record the divisional designated patent application as adapted by the *Patents (General) Rules*.[78] Thus, the same application form is used as for a normal application but the form will indicate the details of the earlier request to record. The date of compliance with the formality requirements are based on the actual date of filing of the new request to record and not on the date of filing of the earlier request to record.

Further Processing of Applications and Restoration of Rights

Introduction

In the event of an application being refused or deemed withdrawn as a result of a failure to comply with time limits set in Part II of the *Patents Ordinance* including any time limit set by the Registrar, an applicant may in certain circumstances apply for reinstatement of the application[79] or restoration of his rights[80] lost by any such refusal or deemed withdrawal.

On application for further processing the Registrar will reinstate the application for the standard patent if the notice is in order but on restoration of rights the Registrar may exercise discretion and restore the application only if he is satisfied that the failure to comply occurred in spite of the applicant having taken all reasonable care under the circumstances.

Further processing of an application for a standard patent

If an application for a standard patent is refused or deemed withdrawn as a result of a failure by the applicant to comply with a time limit, such applicant may apply for reinstatement of the application to its former status.

An application must be made by giving notice to the Registrar

- in writing on the form specified by the Registrar;[81]
- within two months after the application is refused or deemed withdrawn;
- together with an additional fee; and
- make good any deficiency in the filing requirements.

If all the above requirements are met within two months after the application is refused or deemed withdrawn the Registrar will reinstate the application.

There is no right to apply for further processing where the application is refused or deemed withdrawn as a result of:

- Failure to pay the filing fee and the advertisement fee on filing the request to record or the request for registration and grant within the times set or within the further grace period;
- Failure to file any part of the request for registration and grant within the relevant six months period for the purposes of obtaining a filing date; and
- Failure to make good the deficiencies in the minimum requirements in filing the request for registration and grant.

There is no right to apply for further processing in respect of a failure to file any part of the request to record within the relevant six-month period for the purposes of obtaining a filing date or failure to make good the deficiencies in the minimum requirements in filing the request to record. In these cases the request to record is not considered to be an application.

Restoration of rights

An applicant may apply to the Registrar to restore rights lost by a refusal or deemed withdrawal of the application of the standard patent as a result of a failure to comply with a time limit. Such application for restoration must be made to the Registrar not later than one year after the expiry of the time limit in question or two months after the removal of the cause of non-compliance whichever is the earlier. It must be made

- in writing on the form specified by the Registrar;[82]
- with the additional fee; and

- must make good the deficiency in the filing requirement.

Thus up to one year after the application is refused or deemed withdrawn, an applicant may apply for restoration if the deficiency can be made good. This application must be made within two months of the removal of the cause of non-compliance.

The Registrar will consider any such application and if he is satisfied that the failure to comply with the time limit occurred in spite of the applicant having taken all reasonable care under the circumstances, may restore the rights lost by the refusal or deemed withdrawal.

These are new provisions and the cases in which such restoration will be granted cannot be predicted. The provisions are closer to the European Patent Convention than the similar provisions in the *Patents Act* 1977. The Registrar is likely to consider relevant precedents from other jurisdictions in reaching a decision for restoration.

If an order for restoration is made certain rights are preserved for third parties to continue action done or commenced by them in good faith on the belief that the application had lapsed. Such acts will not constitute an infringement of the applicant's rights.

There is no right to apply for restoration of rights for failure to comply with time limit in respect of:[83]

- The filing requirements for the request to record except in relation to the translation requirements;
- The making good of deficiencies in the filing requirements for a request to record;
- The filing requirements for making a divisional application;
- Failure to pay the filing fee and the advertisement fee on filing the request for registration and grant within the times set or within the further grace period;
- Failure to file any part of the request for registration and grant within the relevant six month period for the purposes of obtaining a filing date; and
- Failure to make good the deficiencies in the minimum requirements in filing the request for registration and grant.

Diary reminder for making good deficiencies

The filing requirements should be made good within the times set by the Registrar.

If the application for a standard patent is refused or deemed withdrawn due to a failure to comply with a time limit, application may be made for further processing within two months after the refusal or deemed withdrawal.

If the application for a standard patent is refused or deemed withdrawn due to a failure to comply with a time limit, application for restoration of rights may be made in special circumstances within 12 months after the expiry of the time limit or within two months after the removal of the cause of non-compliance with the time limit, whichever is earlier.

The right to apply for further processing or restoration of rights is limited.

Summary of Application Procedures

Patents Ordinance

Part II and III of the *Patents Ordinance* deals with the application procedures.

Sections 12 to 14 set out persons who may apply for a standard patent and the determination of questions before grant on application to the court or to the Registrar.

Sections 15 to 22 contain the detailed provisions for making the application at the first stage including the documents to be filed, the minimum requirements for obtaining a filing date, the detail of examination by the Registrar and making good any deficiencies in the application, the recording of the request to record and its publication.

Sections 23 to 27 similarly contain the detailed provisions for making the application at the second stage and for the grant and publication of the standard patent .

Sections 28 and 29 contains the provisions to deal with reactivation or restoration where an application is refused or deemed withdrawn because of a failure to comply with a time limit.

Sections 31 to 32 and 36 deal with amendments and the withdrawal at the request of the applicant of a standard patent application before grant.

Sections 33 to 35 set out the requirements for the maintenance of a standard patent application and for restoration in the event of failure to maintain.

Section 37 gives the Registrar the right to refuse to record or register a request if he considers the subject matter of the patent is not patentable because it is contrary to *ordre public* or morality.

Outline of procedures

Application at the first stage is made by filing an application for a request to record the designated patent application. A filing date will be accorded after minimum requirements are complied with. After a formality check the Registrar will record the request in the register and publish this and advertise notice of the grant in the Gazette. Once the request to record is published it is considered to be a published application for a standard patent

Application at the second stage is made by filing an application to request to register the corresponding designated patent and to grant the standard patent. A date of filing will be accorded after minimum requirements are complied with. After the formalities are complied with the Registrar will register the designated patent and grant the standard patent, publish it and advertise notice of the grant in the Gazette.

Outline of formality requirements

The Registrar is required only to ensure that the formal requirements of the application procedure are complied with. The formality procedures follow the methodology used in the European Patent Convention. The Hong Kong Patents Registry will as a first step examine whether the minimum requirements are complied with and if so accord a filing date. Once the filing date is given an examination as to the formal requirements is carried out.

Applicants are given time in which to comply with the requirements. Applicants will be given a period of two months after notification which can be extended for a further period of up to six months. There are provisions which allow for further processing and restitution of rights in certain circumstances. These formality procedures apply to both stages of the application procedure.

Notes

1 See Chapters 2 and 3.

2 Section 10 *Patents Ordinance.*

3 Patents (General) Rules and Notice of Specification of Forms.

4 Sections 2 and 6(1) *Patents Ordinance.*

5 Sections 3 and 27 *Patents Ordinance.*

6 Section 7 *Patents Ordinance.*

7 Sections 15 and 23 *Patents Ordinance.*

8 Section 140 *Patents Ordinance.*

9 Section 85 *Patents (General) Rules.*

10 Form P17 Version 6.97.

11 Section 140 *Patents Ordinance.*

12 Section 31 *Patents Ordinance.*

13 Section 27 *Patents (General) Rules.*

14 Section 32 *Patents Ordinance.*

15 Section 37 *Patents Ordinance.*

16 Section 12 *Patents Ordinance.*

17 Sections 12-14 *Patents Ordinance.*

18 Sections 3-7 *Patents (General) Rules.*

19 Section 13 *Patents Ordinance.*

20 Section 42 and 55 *Patents Ordinance.*

21 Section 15 *Patents (General) Rules.*

22 Section 15(1) *Patents Ordinance.*

23 Section 16(a) *Patents Ordinance* and s 15 *Patents (General) Rules.*

24 Sections 8-15 Patents (General) Rules.

25 Section 15(2) *Patents Ordinance* and ss 8-10 *Patents (General) Rules.*

26 Form P4 Version 06.97.

27 Sections 22 or 55 *Patents Ordinance.*

28 Section 15(2)(e) *Patents Ordinance.*

29 Section 15(2)(b) *Patents Ordinance.*

30 Section 15(2)(f) *Patents Ordinance* and s 10 *Patents (General) Rules.*

31 Section 15(2) *Patents Ordinance.*

32 Section 15(2)(a) *Patents Ordinance.*

33 Section 8(2)(a)(i) *Patents (General) Rules.*

34 Patents Steering Committee Report para 10.9.

35 Patents Steering Committee Report p 105.

36 Section 15(2)(d) *Patents Ordinance* and s 9 *Patents (General) Rules.*

37 Section 8 (2)(f) and s 56 *Patents (General) Rules.*

38 As at 27 June 1997 the fee for filing a request to record is HK$1,400 and the advertisement fee as published in the Gazette on the 27 June 1997 is HK$4,800.

39 Section 16(a)(i) *Patents Ordinance.*

40 Section 8(2)(d) *Patents (General) Rules.*

41 Section 56(2) *Patents (General) Rules.*

42 Section 16(c) *Patents Ordinance.*

43 Section 15(2) and s 16(b) and (c) *Patents Ordinance.*

44 Section 15(2)(b) *Patents (General) Rules.*

45 Section 8(2)(a) *Patents (General) Rules.*

46 Section 9(a) *Patents (General) Rules.*

47 Section 56(3) *Patents (General) Rules.*

48 Sections 17 & 18 *Patents Ordinance.*

49 Sections 19 & 20 *Patents Ordinance.*

50 Sections 28 & 29 *Patents Ordinance.*

51 Section 17 *Patents Ordinance.*

52 Section 16 *Patents (General) Rules.*

53 Section 100 *Patents (General) Rules.*

54 Section 11 *Patents (General) Rules.*

55 Section 28(3) *Patents Ordinance.*

56 Section 17(1) *Patents (General) Rules.*

57 Section 17 *Patents (General) Rules.*

58 Section 17(4) *Patents (General) Rules.*

59 Speech of Averil C Waters dated 17 July 1996 at a seminar on Intellectual Property Law and Practice organised by Law Seminars Ltd, Hong Kong.

60 Section 20 *Patents Ordinance.*

61 Section 20(3) *Patents Ordinance.*

62 Section 23(1) *Patents Ordinance.*

63 Section 23 *Patents Ordinance,* s 19 *Patents (General) Rules* and Form P5 Version 06.97 Notice of Specification of Forms.

64 Section 23(3)(a) *Patents Ordinance.*

65 Section 102 *Patents (General) Rules.*

66 Section 19(2) *Patents (General) Rules.*

67 Section 23(3) *Patents Ordinance* and ss 19 and 20 P*atents (General) Rules.*

68 Fees set on 27 June 1997 by Schedule 1 P*atents (General) Rules* are Fee No 3 as $1400 and Fee No 7 being the advertisement fee set at $2040.

69 Section 25 *Patents Ordinance.*

70 Section 23 *Patents (General) Rules.*

71 Section 23 *Patents (General) Rules.*

72 Section 25 *Patents Ordinance.*

73 Section 21 *Patents (General) Rules.*

74 Section 24 *Patents (General) Rules.*

75 Section 24(4) *Patents (General) Rules.*

76 Section 27 *Patents Ordinance.*

77 Section 22 *Patents Ordinance.*

78 Section 18 *Patents (General) Rules.*

79 Section 28 *Patents Ordinance.*

80 Section 29 *Patents Ordinance.*

81 Section 25 *Patents (General) Rules* and Form P13 Version 06.97.

82 Section 26 *Patents (General) Rules* and Form P13 Version 06.97.

83 Section 29(5) *Patents Ordinance.*

10 Short-term Patents

The new law provides for a new form of protection for inventions with a short-term commercial life. Although these inventions may warrant protection under the patent system, inventors or businessmen wishing to exploit an invention with only a short-term commercial life usually require protection which is quicker and less expensive to obtain than the standard patent.

In line with the recommendations of the Patents Steering Committee the new law attempts to achieve an appropriate balance between the needs of the inventor and the public. The new law provides for a non-examination system which in practical terms means that the short-term patent will be granted after a formality examination only. Because there will be no examination of the prior art or for inventiveness some additional safeguards are introduced by the new law to prevent the potential for abuse.

Costs of Obtaining and Maintaining a Short-term Patent

An applicant for a short-term patent will have to file the same type of documents as required for the standard patent. Thus an applicant for a short-term patent will have to prepare and file a specification which must comply with the formal requirements of the new law and include claims, description and drawings if any, and an abstract of the invention.

It will be just as important for applicants for a short-term patent as for a standard patent to frame the specification carefully and applicants will be well advised to instruct qualified agents to act on their behalf.

The applicant will also have to obtain a search report from a prescribed searching authority. This will be an additional expense and concerns have been expressed that the costs of such a search report may deter applicants from applying for a short-term patent. The ability to defer grant for up to 12 months and to defer filing the search report until the end of the deferment period is intended to address these concerns.

Taking account of the costs of preparing and filing the specification and of obtaining a search report, it is likely that at the initial stages the cost of applying for a standard patent and a short-term patent will not differ substantially. However the costs of prosecuting the application through the Hong Kong Patents Registry will be substantially less and the process quicker.

Because the patent will not be examined prior to grant, the courts will have to consider the validity of the short-term patent without the benefit of knowing that it has been through the examination process.

Under the provisions of the new law the proprietor of the patent will be required to establish *prima facie* the validity of the patent.[1] It can be expected that the costs of enforcing a patent may be greater in respect of a short-term patent and the proprietor will not have the same certainty in relying on the protection afforded by the short-term patent as he would have if the patent is granted after full search and examination.

Time for Obtaining Grant of a Short-term Patent

The short-term patent will be granted after compliance with the formality requirements. If the applicant complies with these requirements it is expected that a short-term patent can be granted within three to four months after the application is lodged. An applicant who wishes to defer the grant may do so for a period of up to 12 months provided he requests this at the time of filing the application.[2]

In summary, under the short-term patent system it is possible to obtain protection much more quickly and more simply than under the main system.

Application for a Short-term Patent

Application for a short-term patent will be made to the Hong Kong Patents Registry. The applicant will have to file an application form, a specification which will include a description, one independent claim and drawings (if any) and an abstract. In addition, an applicant will have to file a search report from a prescribed searching authority.[3]

As a safeguard against abuse only one independent claim and relevant number of subsidiary claims can be validly made. The fact that more than one independent claim is made should not affect the granting of a short-term patent, but only one independent claim will be considered the subject of the invention.[4]

Application for a short-term patent can be made to the Hong Kong Patents Registry either as a domestic application or one that is based on an international application.[5]

An international application is an application for a patent or utility model made under the PCT. The PCT provides for an international application to be made to a receiving office designating a country which is a member state. The receiving office is the office of one of the member states of the PCT authorised to receive international applications or the International Bureau of the World Intellectual Property Organisation. If a country is designated in the international application then entry into the national or domestic phase occurs after notification by the applicant and with minimum formality requirements.

An application for a short-term patent can be based on an international application seeking a patent for a utility model which has designated a utility model in China. Thus, once the international application for a utility model designating China has entered the national phase in China, application for a short-term patent can be made in Hong Kong by filing an application for an short-term patent in Hong Kong within six months of the entry into the national phase in the Chinese Patent Office.

The filing requirements on application are simpler. An applicant can file a photocopy of the international application and the international search report in place of filing a fresh specification and separate search report. Once the application for a short-term patent is filed the requirements of the patent law in Hong Kong must be complied with in order to obtain the short-term patent. Once the short-term patent is granted the date of filing for the purposes of the *Patents Ordinance* is deemed to be the date of filing of the international application. It must be emphasised that the application, even though based on an international application, is not a registration of the utility model patent granted by the Chinese Patent Office and the applicant is not required to file the granted utility model patent.

The application requirements for applying for a short-term patent set out in the *Patents Ordinance* follows international standards for making an application for a patent. For this reason the documentation to be filed will be substantially the same as the underlying documentation which will in fact be filed to obtain a standard patent. This will ensure that searchers can obtain full information about the short-term patent once it is granted.

Search report

A search report given by one of the approved searching authorities as set out in the Rules must be filed on an application for a short-term patent. These authorities are the International Searching Authorities approved by the Assembly of the PCT and the three designated patent offices.[6] This search report must be the report of a search carried out by such authority in respect of the prior art in relation to the invention. The search must be based on the claims and have due regard to the description and drawings.[7] The *Patents (General) Rules* sets out the detailed information to be supplied on the search report.[8] If application for deferment is made the search report may be filed at any time up to one month before the end of the deferment period.[9]

Priority right

An applicant in Hong Kong for a short-term patent can claim a right of priority based on a patent applied for in a Paris Convention country or a World Trade Organisation country, territory or area.[10]

Standard and level of patentability

Under the new law the same standard and level of patentability for the invention applies to both the short-term patent and the standard patent. There are no differences in this respect between the two types of patents.

General provisions

The term of the short-term patent will be eight years renewable after four years.[11] The rights and remedies given to the proprietor of the short-term patent on grant will be the same as those given to the proprietor of the standard patent.

An application for a short-term patent may be filed in English or Chinese but if the name of the applicant is given in Chinese characters a transliteration must also be provided in the roman alphabet. The abstract and the title of the invention must be provided in both English and Chinese.

Special provisions

In order to provide some protection against the potential for abuse which can arise out of a non-examination system the new law introduces some specific provisions in court proceedings for the enforcement of the short-term patent.[12]

Under these provisions the proprietor of the patent is required in any court proceedings to establish *prima facie* the validity of the patent. In addition, if in any interlocutory proceedings before the court an order is made with regard to the short-term patent either party has the right to apply to the court for an order for a speedy trial.

Summary

The key aspects of the short-term patent are as follows:

- Application is made to the Hong Kong Patents Registry for the grant of a short-term patent directly or, where application is based on an international application under the PCT, within six months after the entry into the national phase in the Chinese Patent Office;
- Application must be supported by a specification setting out the claims, description and drawings (if any) of the invention;
- The title of the invention and the abstract must be filed in English and Chinese;
- A search report issued by a prescribed searching authority or, in the case of an international application, the international search report must be filed before grant of the short-term patent;
- An applicant may on application request the deferment of the grant of the short-term patent for up to 12 months;
- An international application designating China and seeking a patent for a utility model may be the basis for an application for a short-term patent;

- The short-term patent will be granted once the formality requirements are in order;
- Paris Convention priority can be claimed;
- The term is eight years renewable after four years; and
- Special provisions exist in respect of court proceedings.

Proposed New Law

The provisions which relate only to a short-term patent are contained in Part XV of the *Patents Ordinance*. Sections 108 to 112 deal with the right to apply for a short-term patent , patentability and priority. Sections 113 to 125 deal with applications for a short-term patent and the procedure up to and including grant. Sections 126 to 128 deal with provisions as to short-term patents after grant.

Part 1 of the *Patents Ordinance* which covers the definitions is also relevant to short-term patents. Details of the definitions are set out in Chapter 8.

Parts IV-VII, IX-XIV, XVI-XVIII and some parts of Part XIX and Schedules 1 and 2 apply to a short-term patent subject to some adaptation.

The detail of the procedures is covered by the *Patents (General) Rules* made under s 149 *Patents Ordinance* by the Registrar.[13] The forms to be used have been specified by the Registrar and published in the Gazette.[14]

Meaning of terms used and other aspects

It is necessary to consider some of the terms used and some other general points before moving on to outline the actual application procedures. Part I of the *Patents Ordinance* contains the main definitions of the terms used in Part XV. Those that are of particular relevance to an short-term patent are highlighted below.

The term *patent* has been defined to include both a standard patent and a short-term patent. A short-term patent has been defined as a patent for an invention granted under Part XV.[15]

A *short-term patent application* is defined as an application under Part XV for a short-term patent.[16]

The term *date of filing* in relation to a short-term patent means the date of filing given to the application by the Registrar after compliance with the minimum formality requirements.[17] However, in the case of an application based on an international application which results in the grant of a short-term patent, the application shall be deemed to have as its date of filing the international filing date accorded to the international application for the purposes of Article 11 of the PCT.[18] Thus, for the purposes of establishing novelty and rights to a patent the relevant date is the international filing date or the date of priority.

The meaning of the term *published* depends on the context in which it appears. The term published under the *Patents Ordinance* for the purposes of the application procedures for a short-term patent under Part XV means any document which can be inspected as of right in Hong Kong.[19] Thus, unless the context otherwise requires, reference to a short-term patent being published is reference to it being published on grant under s 118 of the *Patents Ordinance*. The meaning of the term *published* under s 5(2)(e) of the *Patents Ordinance* should have no effect on the interpretation of the term *published* under s 5(1) of the *Patents Ordinance* for the purposes of establishing novelty of an international application which has been published by the International Bureau of the World Intellectual Property Organisation under the PCT.

The new law confirms a general principle of registration procedures, namely, that filing a document will only be considered as completed when the fee is paid.[20]

The new law makes it clear that the Registrar is only required to carry out an examination to ensure that the application complies with the formal requirements and is not required to carry out any substantive search or examination.[21]

Any act or procedure which under the *Patents Ordinance* can be done by any person may be done by a duly authorised agent of such person. Such authorisation may be in writing or given orally.[22] These provisions apply equally to both short-term patents and standard patents.

The *Patents (General) Rules* deals with the specifics but it is not anticipated that there will be any necessity to file evidence of such authorisation except where the Registrar has some doubts as to the authority of the agent to act. In addition, the Registrar may request such evidence where, during any procedures or proceedings before the Registrar, there is a first appointment of an agent or where there is a change in the agent. This reflects the current law and practice in Hong Kong in respect of both trade mark and patent registration.

Amendment and withdrawal of application for short-term patent

An application for a short-term patent may be amended by the applicant on his own volition at any time before the grant of the patent or before preparations for publication have been completed.[23] Such amendment must not extend the subject-matter as disclosed in the application as filed.[24] An application for amendment must be made in the specified form set in the *Patents (General) Rules*.[25]

An applicant for short-term patent may withdraw his application at any time. Such withdrawal cannot be revoked.[26] No withdrawal, amendment of an application or filing of a divisional short-term patent application can be made after the date on which preparations for the publication of the short-term patent have been completed.[27]

Micro-organisms

In the case where the specification requires for its performance the use of a micro-organism, the *Patents Ordinance* contains provisions allowing for Rules to be made prescribing the circumstances in which the specification of a short-term patent is to be treated as disclosing the invention.[28] The *Patents (General) Rules* sets out the steps required to make available samples of the micro-organism and the conditions under which the invention will be treated as being disclosed.[29] These conditions include the information which must be supplied on filing the application in relation to the deposit of the cultures and the provisions for making the deposited cultures available.

Registrar may refuse to grant a short-term patent

The Registrar may refuse to grant a short-term patent if he considers the invention which is the subject of the application for the short-term patent is not a patentable invention because the working of the invention would be contrary to *ordre public* or morality. Such working shall not be deemed to be so contrary merely because is prohibited by any law in force in Hong Kong.[30] The Registrar must give the applicant a right to be heard before refusing the grant of the short-term patent.[31]

Right to apply for a short-term patent

The new law differentiates between who may apply for the patent and who may in fact be entitled to obtain the short-term patent in

Hong Kong. This follows the method used in the 1977 Act. Thus any person may apply for a short-term patent.[32]

Unlike the provisions for a standard patent, it is not possible under the *Patents Ordinance* for the question of who may apply in Hong Kong for a short-term patent to be considered and determined before the grant of the patent. Questions on entitlement can only be considered on application to the court either after grant under the provisions of the *Patents Ordinance* or if appropriate, before grant under the inherent jurisdiction of the court to determine such questions.

Priority right

Part XV gives a person, who has applied for a patent in any Paris Convention country or in a country territory or area which is a member of the World Trade Organisation and which is listed in Schedule 1 of the *Patents Ordinance*, a right of priority for the period of 12 months after the date of filing the first application for the purpose of filing an application for a short-term patent in Hong Kong.[33]

The effect of the right of priority is that the date of priority of the first application will be considered as the date of priority of the filing of the short-term patent application in Hong Kong for the purposes of establishing the state-of-the-art and the novelty of the short-term patent.[34]

In order to claim priority the applicant for a short-term patent must claim the priority on filing the application, make a statement of priority and file a copy of the earlier application. Although it is not spelt out these provisions should also apply to a right of priority claimed in respect of an application based on an international application under the PCT whether claimed in the international application or on application in Hong Kong.

Non-prejudicial disclosure

In establishing the novelty of a short-term patent the *Patents Ordinance* contains provisions which ensure that certain disclosures of the invention will be disregarded for the purposes of establishing novelty if they were made within six months of the application.

Disclosures which will be considered as non-prejudicial will be disclosures which are made

- as a result of abuse in relation to the applicant, for example, in breach of confidence or fraud; and
- as a result of a disclosure at an officially recognised International Exhibition falling within the terms of the Convention on International Exhibitions.

The disclosure at an International Exhibition can only be relied upon if this disclosure is claimed at the time of filing the application and a statement and written evidence which establishes such disclosure at a recognised exhibition is filed in support.[35] The *Patents Ordinance* is quite clear that only the disclosure at an International Exhibition is required to be claimed and s 70 *Patents (General) Rules* refers only to the requirement to file evidence when there has been a disclosure at an international exhibition.

However, s 58(5)(e) *Patents (General) Rules* requires an applicant to give information on a disclosure as a result of a breach of confidence on filing. In the unlikely event that information relating to a disclosure as a result of a breach of confidence is available at that time of filing, the failure to disclose this at the time of filing should not affect the validity of the patent.

Application for a Short-term Patent

Application for a short-term patent under the new law can be made after the commencement date of the new law.[36]

Filing requirements – the relevant sections

The formal filing requirements for making an application are set out in s 113 of the *Patents Ordinance* and ss 54 and 58 to 62 *Patents (General) Rules*.

Any person may make an application to the Registrar for a standard patent by filing a request for the grant of the short-term patent. The application may be made by the applicant or his agent and may be made in either English or Chinese. The application may be made, based on an international application under the PCT for a patent for a utility model designating China, within six months after the international application has entered the national phase in China.[37]

The documents to be filed in making the application for a short-term patent and the information to be given in support which will together constitute the formal requirements for making an application will be

- an application form;
- certain documents in support; and
- a filing fee and advertising fee.

Application form

An application form[38] will have to be filed. This form has been specified by the Registrar under s 150 of the *Patents Ordinance* in the Notice of Specification of Forms.[39] The form is available in English or Chinese and must be completed in the language the applicant wishes to use as the language of the proceedings. Thus, the language which is used on the form will be the language of the proceedings. The form must be signed by the applicant or his agent.

The following information must be given on the form:

- The reference of the applicant's agent;
- The name and address of the applicant which may be given in English or Chinese but if the name is given in Chinese characters a transliteration of the name must also be given in the roman alphabet;
- The title of the invention which should be short and indicate the matter to which the patent relates;
- The classification of the invention according to the International Patent Classification up to the subclass level and also indicating the edition number of the IPC used;[40]
- If the invention requires the use of a micro-organism for its performance, details of the
  - (i) depository institution;
  - (ii) date of deposit with such institution; and
  - (iii) accession number of the deposit;
- If the application for a short-term patent is based on an international application the following information is required:
  - (i) international application number given by the International Bureau of the World Intellectual Property Organisation;
  - (ii) the international filing date accorded to the international application;

(iii) the publication number of the international application allocated by the International Bureau of the World Intellectual Property Organisation;
(iv) the date of entry into the national phase in the Chinese Patent Office of the international application;
(v) the date of issuance of the National Application Notification by the Chinese Patent Office (if applicable); and
(vi) the application number of the Chinese patent application (if known);

- If the application is divided or is derived from an earlier Hong Kong application then the relevant section of the *Patents Ordinance* under which application is made must be stated[41] together with the following information:
  (i) the earlier application number in Hong Kong; and
  (ii) the date of filing of the earlier application in Hong Kong;
- If the benefit of the right of priority accorded in the designated patent office is to be claimed under s 111 of the *Patents Ordinance*,[42] then the form must state this and give
  (i) the country in which priority is claimed;
  (ii) the application number of the prior application on which the application for priority is claimed; and
  (iii) the date of filing of such prior application;
- The name and the last known address of the person the applicant believes to be the inventor.[43] If the name of the inventor is only given in Chinese characters a transliteration of the name must also be given in the roman alphabet;
- If a claim under s 109 *Patents Ordinance* is made in the designated patent application in respect of any non-prejudicial disclosure and it is wished to claim the benefit in Hong Kong then the form must state this and give the following information in respect of the claim:[44]
  (i) the name and place of the exhibition;
  (ii) the opening date of such exhibition; and
  (iii) the date of the first disclosure of the invention;
- Indicate if a request for deferral is made and the period for which deferral is required. If this is not specifically stated it will be taken that a deferral is not requested;
- The form must state the documents in support and the number of sheets of these documents. This is an administrative requirement;

- The name and address of the applicant's agent, if any, and an address for service in Hong Kong if the applicant does not have an address in Hong Kong; and
- A request to grant a short-term patent.

Documents in support

The following documents are to be filed in support of the application:[45]

- The specification which shall contain[46]
  - (i) the description;
  - (ii) the claim or claims; and
  - (iii) the drawings (if any);
- An abstract of the invention in both English and Chinese which contains a concise summary of the matter contained in the specification and any relevant drawings.[47]
- A verified copy of the previous application on which the claim to priority is based and a translation into the language of the proceedings of such priority documents if they are not in one of the official languages;[48]
- The search report and if it is not in an official language a translation into the language of the proceedings;[49]
- In the case of an application based on an international application, instead of the documents outlined in para 1 above, the following documents are required:
  - (i) a photocopy of the international application as published by the International Bureau of the World Intellectual Property Organisation;
  - (ii) photocopy of the international search report;
  - (iii) photocopy of the translation of the international application if any published by the Chinese Patent Office;
  - (iv) photocopy of any information with regard to the international application published by the Chinese Patent Office; and
  - (v) a copy of the National Application Notification issued by the Chinese Patent Office; and
- A statement of inventorship on the form set in the Rules showing how the applicant derived the right to the patent from the inventor.[50]

Filing fee and advertisement fee

The filing fee and the advertisement fee will be set at different amounts. The advertisement fee is intended to cover the costs of advertising the notice of the publication of the grant of the short-term patent in the Hong Kong Government Gazette. The amounts of these fees are set in Schedule 1 to the *Patents (General) Rules*.[51]

There is provision for a grace period for paying the filing and advertisement fee on filing a request to record. Thus if these fees have not been paid within one month after the date of filing the application for the short-term patent then they may still be validly paid within one month after the Registrar sends notification of the failure to file. This time period cannot be extended and if they are not paid the application will be considered as withdrawn.

Filing requirements for an international application

An application for a short-term patent can be based on an international application seeking a patent for a utility model which has designated a utility model in China. Thus an international application which seeks protection for a utility model patent in China may also be used as the basis for a short-term patent in Hong Kong. In order to use the international route to obtain a short-term patent the international application must designate China and indicate that a utility model patent is sought in China. On completion of the international phase application must be made to enter the national phase in China within the time frames set by the PCT. Once the formality requirements are complied with and the international application has entered the national phase in China, application for a short-term patent must be made in Hong Kong by filing an application for a short-term patent in Hong Kong within six months.

In summary, an international application for the utility model patent is processed in the normal way until it enters into the national phase in China. Once it has entered the national phase application must be made for the short-term patent in Hong Kong within six months.

The application in Hong Kong must be made within six months after the entry into the national phase in China of the international application or such other date as may be prescribed by rules.[52] The other date as specified in the *Patents (General) Rules* is any date within six months after the date of issuance of the National Application Notification by the Chinese Patent Office.[53] The provisions differ from those contained in ss 15 and 16 of the *Patents Ordinance*, which provide for an application for a standard patent application to be made in Hong Kong within six months after the date of publication by the designated patent office of such data as evidences the entry into the national phase rather than the date of entry. It is assumed that in all cases an applicant will rely on the 'other date' as provided in the *Patents (General) Rules* namely the issue of the Application Notification by the Chinese Patent Office as this will allow for a slightly later date than if the date of entry is relied upon. The date of entry is a matter of internal record and is not known until publication or notice is given by the Chinese Patent Office.

The filing requirements on application based on an international application are essentially the same as a domestic application but some aspects are simpler. Thus the same documents with some amendments are required:

- an application form;
- documents in support; and
- filing and advertising fees.

The same application form is used for both a domestic application and an application based on an international application but certain additional information is required to be given on the form in relation to the international application:

- International application number given by the International Bureau of the World Intellectual Property Organisation;
- The international filing date accorded to the international application;
- The publication number of the international application allocated by the International Bureau of the World Intellectual Property Organisation;
- The date of entry into the national phase in the Chinese Patent Office of the international application;
- The date of issuance of the National Application Notification by the Chinese Patent Office (if applicable); and
- The application number of the Chinese patent application (if known).

Some of the documents to be filed in support are different. The differences are highlighted below.

An applicant must file

- a photocopy of the international application and the international search report in place of filing a fresh specification and separate search report;
- a photocopy of the translation of the international application (if any) published by the Chinese Patent Office;
- photocopy of any information published by the Chinese Patent Office;
- a copy of the National Application Notification issued by the Chinese Patent Office; and
- the abstract as contained in the international application which will have to be supplied in both official languages.

The filing and advertising fees are the same for filing an application based on an international application.

Once the application for a short-term patent is filed the formality requirements of the patent law in Hong Kong must be complied with in order to obtain the short-term patent. Once the short-term patent is granted the date of filing for the purposes of the *Patents Ordinance* is deemed to be the date of filing of the international application. It must be emphasised that the application, even though based on an international application, is not a registration of the utility model patent granted by the Chinese Patent Office and the applicant is not required to file the granted utility model patent.

Points to note on the application form

The following matters in relation to the application form are highlighted below.

Title of the invention

A title of the invention will have to be given in the application form in both official languages. The title must be short and indicate the matter to which the invention relates.

Name of the inventor

If the applicant or the applicants are not the inventor, the person whom the applicant believes to be the inventor must be named in the application form.[54] A statement showing how the applicant derives his right to the short-term patent from the inventor must also be filed.

This statement is required to reflect the fact that, although any person may apply for a short-term patent, the person entitled to the grant of the short-term patent is the inventor or his successor in title.

Classification of the invention
The applicant is required to give the designation of the classification of the invention according to the International Patent Classification up to the subclass level. This information will be given by the searching authority.

Micro-organisms
If the invention requires the use of a micro-organism for its performance, information on the deposit of such micro-organism must be given including the name of the depository and the date of deposit.

Priority claim
If priority is to be claimed this must be claimed on making the application. It is important that a claim for priority is made on application and the relevant information given in the application form.

Non-prejudicial disclosure
If a claim for non-prejudicial disclosure based on an exhibition at an international convention is to be made, the fact of that disclosure and the required data is to be given on the application form. It is important to claim this disclosure on application and give the relevant information in the application form.

Request for deferral
A request for deferral of the grant of the short-term patent must be made on application and stated in the application form. If it is not requested on application then it will be taken that deferral is not requested. A request for deferral must state the period for which deferral is required. It is possible to give notice to the Registrar if the applicant wishes to shorten the period but not to extend this. It seems, therefore, that if an applicant wants to defer it may be a practical approach to request the full 12 month period in the application form.

Points to note on documents filed in support

Certain aspects of the documents to be filed in support are highlighted below.

Size and presentation of documents

The *Patents (General) Rules* sets out the requirements for documents making up an application for a short-term patent.[55] All documents must be presented in a manner which allows for direct reproduction by photography, photocopying, photo offset and micro-filming in an unlimited number of copies and for scanning for storage and retrieval by a computer. The *Patents (General) Rules* also details the size, headings and margins of the documents to be filed and the method of describing and portraying mathematical or chemical formula. The documents should be legible and reasonably free from alterations. The documents comprising the international application will be taken as complying with these provisions.

Specification

The *Patents (General) Rules* sets out the provisions for the specification. The specification will state the title of the invention and continue with the description and the claim or claims and drawings (if any). This order must be followed.[56]

The *Patents (General) Rules* sets the requirements for the description which will contain certain information which as far as is possible should be in the order set out.[57] The description shall specify the technical field to which the invention relates and indicate the background art as far as is known to the applicant. This is necessary if it is useful for understanding the invention. The description must disclose the invention as claimed in such a way that the technical problem and its solution can be understood and also state any advantageous effects. If there are any drawings these must briefly be described. At least one way of carrying out the invention must be stated using examples where appropriate and if it is not obvious, the way in which the invention is capable of exploitation in industry should be stated.

The *Patents (General) Rules* sets out the requirements for the drawings and the form and manner in which they are to be presented. The drawings shall not be contained in the description, claims or abstract.[58]

The *Patents (General) Rules* sets out in detail the requirements for the claims.[59] The claims shall define the matter for which protection is sought in terms of the technical features of the invention. Only one independent claim stating the essential features of an invention may be claimed followed by one or more dependent claims concerning particular embodiments of the independent claim.

The claims shall contain a statement indicating the designation of the subject-matter of the invention and those technical features which are necessary for the definition of the claimed subject-matter but which, in combination, form part of the prior art. The claims will also contain a characterizing portion stating the technical features which, in combination with the stated technical features which form part of the prior art, it is desired to protect.

In respect of the technical features of the invention,the claims shall not rely on references to the description or drawings,except where absolutely necessary.

Abstract

An abstract in both English and Chinese will be required. This will not be a minimum requirement to obtain a filing date. The *Patents (General) Rules* sets out the detailed requirements of the abstract.[60] The abstract will commence with a title of the invention. It shall contain a concise summary of the matter contained in the specification. The summary shall indicate the technical field to which the invention belongs and be drafted in a way which allows for a clear understanding of the technical problem, the gist of the solution of the problem and the principal use or uses of the invention. The abstract shall not normally contain more than 150 words or 200 Chinese characters as appropriate.

Copies of the priority documents

If priority is to be claimed a copy of the prior application in a Paris Convention country or World Trade Organisation country territory or area duly verified will be required.[61] As explained below this will not be a minimum requirement to obtain a filing date. The copy of the previous application will have to be verified as a correct copy by the authority which received the application or otherwise verified to the satisfaction of the Registrar. The copy must be accompanied by a certificate issued by that authority stating the date of filing of the previous application.

A translation of the previous application into the language of proceedings will be required if it is not in one of the official languages. However, not all of the specification will have to be so translated and this will be limited to the following:

- the title of the invention;
- the claims;

- the filing date; and
- transliteration of the name of the applicant into the roman alphabet.

If the previous application is an application under the Ordinance the applicant may request the Registrar to include a verified copy with the application on payment of the prescribed fee.

Evidence in support of a claim regarding a non-prejudicial disclosure

If a claim for a non-prejudicial disclosure is made based on exhibition at an officially recognised international exhibition the applicant must file a certificate issued at the exhibition by the authority responsible for holding the exhibition and an identification of the invention duly authenticated by that authority. The certificate must state that the invention was in fact exhibited at the exhibition, the opening date of the exhibition and the date of the first disclosure.[62]

Search report

The search report must be provided by one of the International Searching Authorities appointed under the PCT or one of the designated patent offices. The *Patents (General) Rules* sets out the detail which should be given in the report. Thus the report should

- identify the name of the searching authority issuing the report;
- state the date of the report and the date on which the report was actually completed;
- give the classification of the subject-matter of the invention according to the International Patent Classification;
- give the citations of the documents considered to be relevant;
- list the classification identification of the fields searched; and
- give the name of the officer of the searching authority responsible for the report.

Statement of inventorship

Where the applicant is not the inventor a statement in the form set out in the *Patents (General) Rules* must also be filed.[63] The statement shall give details of the applicant, the person whom the applicant believes to be the inventor and the last known address for that person and state how the applicant derived the right from the inventor. This is a simple statement and evidence in support is not required. The applicant must supply sufficient copies for the form to be served by the Registrar on each inventor who is not an applicant.

Formality Examination by the Registrar

Introduction

On receipt of the application for a short-term patent the Registrar will carry out a formality check to see whether the formal requirements have been complied with so that

- a filing date can be given; and
- a short-term patent can be granted.

In order to give a filing date the Registrar will examine the application to see whether it complies with the minimum requirements.[64] If it does not comply with the minimum requirements the Registrar will give a set time in which to comply. If the requirements are not met the application will fail. If they are met the Registrar will give a filing date and will then carry out a further examination to see whether all the formal requirements have been satisfied. If they have then the Registrar will grant the short-term patent.

If the formal requirements are not complied with the Registrar will ask the applicant to make good the deficiencies in a set time. If the deficiencies are made good then the Registrar will grant the short-term patent. Otherwise, the application will be deemed withdrawn.[65]

There are provisions which allow for further processing or the restoration of rights in the event of the failure of the applicant to make good the deficiencies within the times set by the Registrar.[66]

While these provisions are designed to be user friendly, they are also aimed at making sure that the applicant gets a filing date on filing the minimum requirements and that the short-term patent can be granted as soon as possible after the application is made.

Minimum requirements to obtain a filing date for the application

A filing date can be given if the applicant or his agent files with the Registrar[67]

- indication that a short-term patent is being sought;
- information which identifies the applicant; and
- a document which on the face of it appears to be a description of the invention.

In the case of an application based on an international application under the PCT the minimum requirements outlined or part of them must be filed within six months of the date the international application enters the national phase in China or the date of issue of the National Application Notification by the Chinese Patent Office to obtain a filing date. Although this is not specifically spelt out it is implicit in the provisions of s 125 *Patents Ordinance*.

If only part of this information is filed the Registrar cannot give a filing date but he will then send a request to the applicant requesting that the full details are given within a further one month period.[68] If this information is given within that further period then a filing date will be given.

If the full information required to obtain a filing date is not given on filing or within the time allowed by the Registrar, or in the case of an international application outside the set dates, the application will not be considered as an application for a short-term patent.[69] Thus the provisions for further processing and restoration cannot apply.

The payment of the filing and advertising fees is not a minimum requirement. These fees must however be paid within one month of the earliest date of filing the request to record. If the fees are not so paid, these fees, and an additional late payment fee, can still be paid during a further grace period of up to one month. This period is a one month period after the issue by the Registrar of a notification of the failure to pay the fee where such fee can be validly paid.[70]

Thus if only part of the minimum requirements are filed but the full requirements are filed within the additional time allowed by the Registrar the filing fee must be paid within one month of the first filing or within the grace period. The effect of the grace period is that if the minimum requirements have been complied the filing fee or advertising fee can be validly paid within one month after notification by the Registrar of the failure to pay the fee and on payment of the filing and advertising fee and the additional fee.

The provisions for further processing an application for a short-term patent or restoration of rights[71] do not apply to the failure to comply with the filing of the minimum requirements as the application for a short-term patent will not be considered as an application. In addition, these provisions do not apply on the failure to pay the filing fee in the time set or in the further time allowed by the Registrar.[72]

Thus the minimum requirements must be complied with in the times set to get a filing date.

Diary reminder

To obtain a filing date it is important to note that

- the minimum requirements or part of them must be filed with the Registrar;
- the minimum requirements or part of them in the case of an application based on an international application must be filed within six months of entry into the national phase in the Chinese Patent Office or the date of issue of the National Application Notification by the Chinese Patent Office;
- any deficiencies must be made good in the time set by the Registrar;
- the filing fee and advertising fee must be paid within one month of the first filing of any part of the request to record; and
- the times set by the Registrar cannot be extended and the provisions as to further processing and restoration do not apply.

Formality examination

If a filing date has been given and if the filing and advertising fees have been paid the Registrar will carry out a full formality examination[73] to see whether all the filing requirements[74] have been complied with.

If there are deficiencies the Registrar will inform the applicant or his agent of these and ask for them to be made good within two months of the date of the notice of the deficiencies. If the deficiency relates to filing the verified copy and translation of a previous application on which priority is claimed the Registrar must give a period of not less than three months from the date of filing the subsequent application in which to supply these documents.[75] In all cases the time may be extended for a further period of two months on request and on payment of an additional fee.[76]

Special provisions apply where an application for deferral is made. In such a case the applicant may request an extension of time to file the search report up to one month prior to the expiry of the requested deferred date. This extension of time will only be granted if the applicant has complied with all other formal requirements within the normal time periods.[77]

Further periods in which to comply with the requirements may be allowed by the Registrar on request and on payment of a penalty fee where the only deficiency outstanding is the failure to file a translation of the title of the invention, the abstract of the invention or the transliteration of the name of the applicant or the inventor.[78] This does not apply to the filing of translations for other documents required on filing such as translations of the priority documents.

Thus all formality requirements must be filed within the two months set or the additional two month period except that translations of the data into both languages and the search report may be filed later in the circumstances outlined. In addition there are provisions which allow for further processing or restoration.[79]

An application may be reinstated if within two months after the application is refused or deemed withdrawn the applicant requests reinstatement in writing, makes good the outstanding requirements and pays the relevant fees. In addition, it is possible in certain circumstances for the application to be restored. An application for restoration can be made up to one year after the application is refused or deemed withdrawn at the discretion of the Registrar on making good the deficiency and payment of the filing fees. The Registrar will only allow such restoration if he considers that the failure to comply with the time limit occurred in spite of the applicant having taken all reasonable care in the circumstances.

If there are no deficiencies or if notified deficiencies are made good within the times set, the Registrar will proceed to grant the short-term patent and publish this. If the deficiencies are not made good the application will either be refused or if no action is taken to comply with the requirements the application will be deemed withdrawn.

In summary, an applicant has two months after the Registrar gives notice of deficiencies in the filing to comply with the requirements. One extension of two months can be requested on payment of filing fees. In essence, therefore, an applicant has four months after notification in which to make good the filing requirements.

Further time will be allowed to file translations of the abstract and the title of the invention if all other requirements have been filed and special provisions apply for the filing of the search report where a request for deferral of grant is made. No further extensions are allowed but further processing will be allowed if application is filed within two months after the date of refusal or deemed withdrawal.

These time periods are quite tight and rather less generous than originally intended.[80] However, taking account of the nature of the documentation required it should not present difficulties but patent owners need to be aware of the importance of supplying the relevant information within these time frames.

Grant of a Short-term Patent

If the formal requirements of the request to record are met and are found to be in order or if a request for deferral has been made after the period of deferral has expired,[81] the Registrar will, as soon as possible,

- grant the short-term patent;
- issue the certificate of grant;
- enter the particulars of the grant in the register;
- publish the specification of the short-term patent and the name of the proprietor, and if different, the name of the inventor; and
- advertise the fact of such grant in the Hong Kong Government Gazette.

On publication the Registrar will make the specification of the short-term patent and the register available for inspection at the Hong Kong Patents Registry.

Even if the formal requirements are met the Registrar will not grant the short-term patent if the application is withdrawn before completion of preparations for publication[82] or if the Registrar considers that the invention which is the subject of the application is not a patentable invention because it is contrary to *ordre public* or morality.[83]

Deferral of grant of a short-term patent

At the time of making the application, an applicant may request the Registrar, to defer the grant of the short-term patent for a period of not more than twelve months. The applicant may subsequently request a shorter period. The period set in the *Patents Ordinance* was six months but this period was extended to 12 months. This reflected the concerns expressed by practitioners that the costs of obtaining a search report would deter applications for a short-term patent.

An applicant may file the search report at any time up to one month before the deferred date for grant of the short-term patent expires, provided he has complied with all the other formal requirements and has requested an extension of time to do so.

The Registrar will grant the short-term patent when the period of deferment has expired provided all the formal requirements, including the filing of the search report, have been met.

Divisional Applications

The *Patents Ordinance* contains provisions which allow an applicant to make a divisional application for a short-term patent.[84]

The right to make a divisional application gives the applicant for the short-term patent or his successor in title the power to file a new application which is in respect of any part of the subject-matter contained in the earlier short-term patent application.

A key factor to remember in making a divisional application is that such application must not extend the subject matter of the earlier application and if it does the application will be invalid to the extent that it does so extend the earlier subject-matter.

Any such application must comply with the requirements of the *Patents (General) Rules* as to the normal filing requirements, procedures and time limits for applying for a short-term patent.[85] Such application may be filed at any time after the earlier application has been filed but cannot be filed after the earlier application has been refused, withdrawn or deemed withdrawn.

Any divisional application which complies with the requirements will be treated as having as its filing date the date of filing of the earlier short-term patent application and will have the benefit of any priority claimed under the earlier short-term patent application.

Further Processing of Applications and Restoration of Rights

In the event of an application for a short-term patent being refused or deemed withdrawn as a result of a failure to comply with the time limits set in Part XV of the *Patents Ordinance* including any time limit set by the Registrar an applicant may in certain circumstances apply for reinstatement of the application or restoration of his rights lost by any such refusal or deemed withdrawal. The provisions of Part

II of the *Patents Ordinance* are applied to Part XV subject to relevant modifications.[86]

The provisions will therefore be the same for both an application for a short-term patent and a standard patent except that the circumstances in which the rights may be claimed are different.

Accordingly, similar to that of a standard patent, on application for further processing the Registrar will reinstate the application for the short-term patent if the notice is in order. However, the Registrar has the discretion on the restoration of rights and may only restore the application if he is satisfied that the failure to comply occurred in spite of the applicant having taken all reasonable care required by the circumstances.

Further processing of an application for a short-term patent

If an application for short-term patent is refused or deemed withdrawn as a result of a failure by the applicant to comply with a time limit, such applicant may apply for reinstatement of the application to its former status.

An application must be made by giving notice to the Registrar

- in writing on the form specified by the Registrar;
- within two months after the application is refused or deemed withdrawn;
- together with an additional fee; and
- make good any deficiency in the filing requirements.

If all the above requirements are met within two months after the application is refused or deemed withdrawn the Registrar will reinstate the application.

There is no right to apply for further processing where the application is refused or deemed withdrawn as a result of failure to pay the filing fee and the advertising fee within the times set or within the further grace period.

There is no right to apply for further processing in respect of a failure to make good the deficiencies in the minimum requirements in filing the request to record. In this case the application for a short-term patent is not considered to be an application This will apply to the failure to file an application based on an international application within the relevant six months period once the international application has entered the national phase in China.

Restoration of rights

An applicant may apply to the Registrar to restore rights lost by a refusal or deemed withdrawal of the application of the short-term patent as a result of a failure to comply with a time limit. Such application for restoration must be made to the Registrar not later than one year after the expiry of the time limit in question or two months after the removal of the cause of non-compliance, whichever is earlier. It must be made

- in writing on the form specified by the Registrar;
- with the additional fee; and
- must make good the deficiency in the filing requirement.

The Registrar will consider any such application and may restore the rights lost by the refusal or deemed withdrawal if he is satisfied that the failure to comply with the time limit occurred in spite of the applicant having taken all reasonable care required by the circumstances.

If an order for restoration is made certain rights are preserved for third parties to continue action done in good faith in the belief that the application had lapsed. Such acts will not constitute an infringement of the applicant's rights.

There is *no right to apply* for restoration of rights for failure to comply with the time limit in respect of [87]

- the filing requirements for obtaining a filing date except in relation to the translation requirements;
- the filing requirements for making a divisional application;
- failure to pay the filing fee and the advertisement fee on filing an application within the times set or the further grace period; and
- failure to make good the deficiencies in the minimum requirements in filing the request for registration and grant.

Diary reminder for making good deficiencies

The filing requirements should be made good within the times set by the Registrar. Thus all formality requirements must be filed within the two months set by the Registrar or the additional two month period. However translations of the title of the invention or the abstract into both languages and the search report may be filed later in the circumstances outlined.

If the application for a short-term patent is refused or deemed withdrawn due to a failure to comply with a time limit, an application may be made for further processing within two months after the refusal or deemed withdrawal.

If the application for a short-term patent is refused or deemed withdrawn due to a failure to comply with a time limit, an application for restoration of rights may be made in special circumstances within 12 months after the expiry of the time limit or within two months after the removal of the cause of non-compliance with the time limit.

The right to apply for further processing or restoration of rights is limited.

Term of Short-term Patent

A short-term patent will take effect from the date of grant for a term of eight years beginning with the date of filing the short-term patent, subject to renewal after the expiry of the fourth year from the date of filing the application.[88]

The short-term patent will expire at the end of the fourth year unless it is renewed. Renewal takes effect for the remainder of the term.[89]

Application for renewal must be filed within three months before the expiry of the fourth year upon payment of the filing fee.

There is a further period of six months to file the renewal fee. If the renewal fee and an additional fee is paid within that period the Registrar must renew the short-term patent.[90] There are provisions for restoration of a lapsed short-term patent.[91]

Summary of Application Procedures

Patents Ordinance

Part XV of the *Patents Ordinance* deals with the application procedures for a short-term patent.

Section 113 sets out who may apply for a short-term patent.

Sections 114 and 115 contain the provisions relating to non-prejudicial disclosure and priority.

Sections 113 to 118 contain detailed provisions for the application for a short-term patent including the documents to be filed, the minimum requirements for obtaining a filing date, the detail of examination by the Registrar and making good any deficiencies in the application and provisions for making a divisional short-term patent application, the grant of a short-term patent and its publication.

Sections 119 to 123 deal with deferral of grant, amendment of the application before grant, withdrawal, limitations on withdrawal and reactivation or restoration where an application is deemed withdrawn because of a failure to comply with a time limit.

Section 124 gives the Registrar the right to refuse to grant a short-term patent if he considers the subject matter of the patent is not patentable because it is contrary to *ordre public* or morality.

Section 125 deals with an application for a short-term patent based on an international application under the PCT for a utility model and designating China.

Outline of procedures

Application for a short-term patent is made by filing an application for a short-term patent with the Registrar. A filing date will be accorded after minimum requirements are complied with. After a formality check the Registrar will grant the short-term patent, publish this and advertise notice of the grant in the Gazette.

Outline of formality requirements

The Registrar is required only to ensure that the formal requirements of the application procedure is complied with. The Hong Kong Patents Registry will as a first step examine whether the minimum requirements are complied with and if so accord a filing date. Once the filing date is given an examination as to the formal requirements is carried out. Applicants are given time in which to comply with the requirements. Applicants will be given a period of two months after notification which can be extended for a further period of two months. There are provisions which allow for further processing and restitution of rights in certain circumstances.

Filing requirements

On application the following will be required:

- An application form;
- A specification containing the claims, description and drawings, if any;
- An abstract in English and Chinese;

- Certain documents in support including the search report; and
- A filing fee and advertising fee.
  Application may be made in either English or Chinese.

Application form

The application form must be in the specified form, completed in either English or Chinese and contain the following information:

- The reference of the applicant's agent;
- The name and address of the applicant. If the name of the applicant is given in Chinese characters a transliteration of the name must also be given in the roman alphabet;
- The title of the invention in English and Chinese;
- The classification of the invention according to the International Patent Classification up to the subclass level;
- If the invention requires the use of a micro-organism for its performance, specified details of the deposit;
- If the application is based on an international application the specified information relating to the international application and the entry into the national phase in China;
- If the application is divided or derived from an earlier Hong Kong application the specified information;
- If priority is claimed the statement required;
- The name and address of the inventor. If the name of the inventor is given in Chinese characters then a transliteration of the name in the roman alphabet must also be given;
- If a claim is made in respect of any non-prejudicial disclosure the relevant statement;
- Indicate if a request for deferral is made;
- Name and address of the agent, if any;
- Address for service; and
- A request to grant a short-term patent.

Documents in support

The following documents must be filed in support of the application

- The specification which shall contain the claims, description and drawings, if any;

- An abstract of the invention in English and Chinese;
- A verified copy of the previous application on which a claim to priority is based and a translation of the document, if it is not in English or Chinese, into the language of the proceedings;
- The search report;
- If the application is based on an international application, a photocopy of the international application as published by the World Intellectual Property Organisation and a photocopy of the international search report in place of items 1, 2 and 4 and photocopies of specified documents issued or published by the Chinese Patent Office; and
- A statement of inventorship showing how the inventor derived the right to the patent.

Filing fee and advertisement fee

The filing fee and the advertisement fee must be paid within the times set.

Notes

1 Section 129 *Patents Ordinance.*

2 Section 119 and 113 *Patents Ordinance.*

3 Section 113 *Patents Ordinance.*

4 Section 113 *Patents Ordinance.*

5 Section 125 *Patents Ordinance.*

6 Section 71 *Patents (General) Rules.*

7 Section 113(8) *Patents Ordinance* and S 72 *Patents (General) Rules.*

8 Section 72 *Patents (General) Rules.*

9 Section 68(4) *Patents (General) Rules.*

10 Section 110 *Patents Ordinance.*

11 Section 126 *Patents Ordinance.*

12 Section 129 *Patents Ordinance.*

13 Section 149 *Patents Ordinance.*

14 Section 150 *Patents Ordinance* and Notice of Specification of Forms published in the Gazette on 27 June 1997.

15 Sections 2 and 6(1) *Patents Ordinance.*

16 Section 2 *Patents Ordinance.*

17 Section 2 *Patents Ordinance.*

18 Section 125(2) *Patents Ordinance.*

19 Section 5 *Patents Ordinance.*

20 Section 7 *Patents Ordinance.*

21 Section 117 *Patents Ordinance.*

22 Section 140 *Patents Ordinance.*

23 Sections 120 and 121 *Patents Ordinance.*

24 Section 120 *Patents Ordinance.*

25 Section 75 *Patents (General) Rules* and Form P8 Version 06.97.

26 Section 121 *Patents Ordinance.*

27 Section 122 *Patents Ordinance.*

28 Section 128 *Patents Ordinance.*

29 Section 73 and Schedule 1 *Patents (General) Rules.*

30 Section 124 *Patents Ordinance*.

31 Section 135 *Patents Ordinance.*

32 Section 108 *Patents Ordinance.*

33 Section 110 *Patents Ordinance* and Schedule 1.

34 Sections 112 and 94(2) *Patents Ordinance*.

35 Section 109 *Patents Ordinance*.

36 27 June 1997.

37 Section 125 *Patents Ordinance.*

38 Section 113 *Patents Ordinance* and s 58 *Patents (General) Rules.*

39 Form P6 Version 06.97.

40 Section 58(5) *Patents (General) Rules.*

41 Section 116 or 55 *Patents Ordinance*.

42 Section 113(4)(b)(ii)*Patents Ordinance* and ss 58 and 69 *Patents (General) Rules.*

43 Section 113 (2)(b) *Patents Ordinance* and s 58 *Patents (General) Rules.*

44 Section 113(4)(b)(iv) *Patents Ordinance* and ss 58 and 70 *Patents (General) Rules.*

45 Section 113 (2) &(4) *Patents Ordinance* .

46 Sections 58-60 and 64 *Patents (General) Rules.*

47 Section 113 *Patents Ordinance*and ss 56 and 61 *Patents (General) Rules.*

48 Sections 58(5)(c) and 56 *Patents (General) Rules.*

49 Sections 56(1), 58(5)(a), 71 and 72 *Patents (General) Rules.*

50 Section 113(2)(c) *Patents Ordinance* and s 65 *Patents (General) Rules* and Form P7 Version 06.97.

51 As at 27 June 1997 the fee for filing an application for a short-term patent is HK$ 2,800 and the advertisement fee as published in the Gazette on the 27 June 1997 is HK$ 4,800.

52 Section 125(2) *Patents Ordinance.*

53 Section 78 *Patents (General) Rules.*

54 Section 113(2(b) *Patents Ordinance.*

55 Section 62 *Patents (General) Rules.*

56 Section 58 (2) *Patents (General) Rules.*

57 Section 59 *Patents (General) Rules.*

58 Sections 60 and 62(9)(a) *Patents (General) Rules.*

59 Section 64 *Patents (General) Rules.*

60 Section 61 *Patents (General) Rules.*

61 Section 69 *Patents (General) Rules.*

62 Section 70 *Patents (General) Rules.*

63 Section 65 *Patents (General) Rules* and Form P7 Version 06.97 of the Forms Notified by the Registrar under s 150 *Patents Ordinance.*

64 Section 114 *Patents Ordinance.*

65 Section 115 *Patents Ordinance.*

66 Section 123 *Patents Ordinance.*

67 Section 114(2) *Patents Ordinance.*

68 Section 67 *Patents (General) Rules.*

69 Section 114(3) *Patents Ordinance*and s 68(6) *Patents (General) Rules.*

70 Section 68(6) *Patents (General) Rules.*

71 Section 123 *Patents Ordinance* and ss 28 and 29 *Patents Ordinance.*

72 Section 123(2) *Patents Ordinance.*

73 Section 115 *Patents Ordinance.*

74 Sections 113 and 125 *Patents Ordinance.*

75 Section 68(1) *Patents (General) Rules.*

76 Section 68(2) *Patents (General) Rules.*

77 Section 68(4) *Patents (General) Rules.*

78 Section 68(5) *Patents (General) Rules.*

79 Section 123 *Patents Ordinance.*

80 Speech by Averil C. Waters dated 17 July 1996 at a seminar on Intellectual Property Law and Practice organised by Law Seminars Ltd, Hong Kong.

81 Section 118 *Patents Ordinance.*

82 Section 121 *Patents Ordinance.*

83 Section 124 *Patents Ordinance.*

84 Section 116 *Patents Ordinance.*

85 Section 74 *Patents (General) Rules.*

86 Section 123 *Patents Ordinance* and ss 28 and 29 *Patents Ordinance.*

87 Section 123(3) *Patents Ordinance.* Note s 123(3) refers to s 115 *Patents Ordinance.* It is assumed this is an error as this would in effect mean that there were no restoration rights. It is assumed this is meant to refer to s 116 *Patents Ordinance.*

88 Section 126 *Patents Ordinance.*

89 Section 126(2) *Patents Ordinance.*

90 Section 126(5) *Patents Ordinance.*

91 Section 127 *Patents Ordinance.*

SUMMARY

11 The Patent Law

Main Features

- Independent patent law;
- Grant of a standard patent based on registration of patents granted by a designated patent office;
- Initial application to the designated patent office;
- Two-stage application procedure in Hong Kong;
- Formality examination only;
- Grant of a short-term patent;
- Initial application in Hong Kong; and
- Granted only after formality examination.

Proposed Designated Patent Offices

- Chinese Patent Office;
- European Patent Office for patents designating the UK; and
- United Kingdom Patent Office.

Standard Patent Application

- Initial application to designated patent office;
- First stage application in Hong Kong within six months of publication of the patent application in the designated patent office; and
- Second stage application in Hong Kong within six months of the grant of the patent by the designated patent office.

Standard Patent Application
(Filing date in Hong Kong; Deemed date of filing; Priority date)

- Date of filing in Hong Kong given when minimum formality requirements complied with;
- Deemed date of filing is the date of filing in the designated patent office; and
- Priority date, if claimed in Hong Kong, is the priority date accorded in the designated patent office.

Standard Patent – Right to Apply

Primarily applicant for the patent in the designated patent office, or the successor in title to such applicant, or person entitled in preference to such applicant.

Standard Patent Application – Maintenance

- First renewal on the first anniversary of the date of filing in the designated patent office falling five years after the date of publication in Hong Kong; and
- Annually thereafter.

Short-term Patent

(Application in Hong Kong)
- Any person may apply;
- Date of filing accorded after minimum requirements met; and
- Date of priority if claimed.

Term

- Standard patent term is 20 years from date of filing in the designated patent office;
- Subject to renewal after the third year from grant and thereafter annually; and
- Short-term patent term is 8 years subject to renewal at the end of the fourth year.

Rights

- To prevent third parties without consent from making, putting on the market, using or importing a product which is the subject-matter of the patent or from stocking the product for the purpose of putting the product on the market whether in Hong Kong or otherwise;
- To prevent third parties without consent from making, putting on the market, using or importing a product which is obtained directly by a process which is the subject-matter of the patent or from stocking the product for the purpose of putting on the market in Hong Kong or otherwise; and
- To prevent third parties without consent, if the subject-matter of the invention is a process, from using the process or offering the process for use where it is known or obvious to a reasonable person in the circumstances that use of such process is not permitted.

Remedies on Infringement

- Injunction;
- Damages; and
- Delivery up.

Amendment of Patent Specification

- Amendment can be made on application to the court; and
- Special provisions for amendment of a standard patent if the patent has been amended in the designated patent office in opposition or post grant revocation proceedings.

Amendment of Patent Application

- Standard patent application can be amended in specified circumstances; and
- Short-term patent can be amended by the applicant subject to conditions.

Patentable Invention

- New;
- Involve an inventive step; and
- Be industrially applicable.

Priority

- Applicant for a standard patent enjoys the same right of priority, if claimed, as is enjoyed in the designated patent office; and
- Applicant for a short-term patent may enjoy priority based on filing in an earlier Paris Convention country or World Trade Organisation member for the period of 12 months after the first filing.

Right to Standard and Short-term Patent

- Inventor or his successor in title; or
- If two or more persons create an invention independently then the person who has the first date of filing or, if claimed, the date of priority in a designated patent office or in the Hong Kong Patents Registry.

Revocation and Putting Validity in Issue

- Invention is not patentable;
- The patent was granted to a person not entitled;
- The subject matter of the patent extends beyond that disclosed in the application for the patent as filed;
- The subject matter has been extended on amendment;
- Specification does not disclose the invention sufficiently clearly to be performed by a person skilled in the art; and
- Double patenting in specified circumstances.

Additional Provisions for Revocation

- Special provisions for revocation of the standard patent after prescribed opposition proceedings in the designated patent office; and
- On application to the Registrar on the ground that the invention is contrary to ordre public or morality.

Compulsory Licensing

- Any person may apply three years after grant on the grounds specified; and
- Court may grant if satisfied the specified conditions are met.

Government Use

- Applies if a period of extreme urgency is declared by the Chief Executive-in-Council;
- Subject to reasonable remuneration for the owner of the patent; and
- Subject to review of the court.

Nature of Patent and Applications

- Patent and application for a patent is personal property;
- Patent or application can be dealt with as personal property, ie transferred, charged and licensed;
- Dealings with patent and application are to be recorded with the Registrar; and
- Special provisions to encourage prompt filing.

Language

- Application for a patent may be made in either official language namely English or Chinese;
- Some data to be provided in both languages;
- Authentic text will be the text in the language of the proceedings before the Registrar; and
- Special provisions for the authentic text in relation to standard patents.

Proceedings Before the Court

- Applications for revocation, amendment and entitlement to the patent;
- Infringement proceedings;
- Putting validity in issue;
- Determination of questions before grant;
- Grant of compulsory licence; and
- Review of government use.

Proceedings Before the Registrar

- Registrar must give any person a right to be heard before exercising a discretion;
- applications for revocation or refusal of a patent on the ground that the invention is contrary to ordre public;
- determination of questions before grant of who may apply for a standard patent;
- Registrar may refer any proceedings to the court; and
- appeal to the High Court from any decision.

Court Proceedings

- Reversal of burden of proof where the invention for which the patent is granted is a process for obtaining a patent;
- In relation to a short-term patent: proprietor of short-term patent must in any court proceedings establish *prima facie* the validity of the short-term patent; and
- In relation to a short-term patent: in any interlocutory proceedings either party may call for a speedy trial.

Agents

- Any act or procedure can be done by the person applying or a duly authorised agent; and
- any person may act as an agent.

12 Transitional Provisions

Background

- Ensure continued protection of patents registered under the old law; and
- Allow for continued protection of patents which could have been protected under the old law but cannot be protected under the new law.

Main Provisions

- All existing registered patents in force in the United Kingdom on the commencement date to be automatically deemed standard patents; and
- Application for grant of standard patent based on United Kingdom and European (UK) patents granted before the commencement date and patents granted after the commencement date as a result of an application for a UK or EP(UK) patent made and published before the commencement date.

Categories of Patents or Applications

- Existing 1949 or 1977 Act registered patents;
- Pending applications for registration under the old law;
- Existing 1949 or 1977 Act patents;
- Published applications for a 1977 Act patent; and
- Existing applications for a 1949 Act patent.

Existing 1949 and 1977Act Registered Patents

- Definition: a patent registered under the current law which is in force in the United Kingdom on the commencement date;
- Deemed to be a standard patent under the new law;
- Term will be 20 years subject to renewal; and
- First renewal on the anniversary of date of filing falling after 27 June 2000 (namely after the end of the third year after the commencement date); thereafter annually.

Pending Applications Under the Old Law

- Definition: a pending application for registration at the commencement date;
- Continue to be processed under the new law; and
- On registration will be considered an existing registered patent.

Existing 1949 or 1977Act Patents

- Definition: patent granted prior to the commencement date by the United Kingdom (including European (UK)), and still capable of being registered under the current law, ie within five years of grant but not yet registered; and
- Under the new law application can be made for a standard patent provided it is made within set time (namely before 27 June 1998) and complies with procedural requirements.

Published Application for a 1977Act Patent

- Definition: an application made for a United Kingdom or a European(UK) patent published prior to the commencement date; and
- Application can be made for a standard patent provided it is within the set time (namely before 7 December 1998) and the procedures are met.

Existing Application for a 1949 Act Patent

- Definition: an application for a United Kingdom patent under the 1949 Act and which at the commencement date is still pending, and for which a patent has not been granted; and
- Application for a standard patent can be made after the 1949 Act patent is granted provided it is made within the set time and complies with the procedures.

1949 Act Patent

- Patents granted under the United Kingdom Patents Act 1949;
- Some provisions of the new law will apply;
- Special provisions are included to ensure continued validity; and
- All 1949 Act patents will expire on 1 June 1998.

1977 Act Patent

- Patents granted under the Patents Act 1977 including European Patents designating the United Kingdom; and
- Provisions of the new law will apply in the main to standard patents based on patents granted under the 1977 Act subject to some modifications.

Application of the New Law to Transitional Standard Patents Based on the 1977 Act

- The provisions relating to employees inventions will not apply;
- The following provisions subject to some modification if necessary will apply:
    - rights and remedies given by the new law;
    - application procedures (if necessary);
    - revocation provisions;
    - patentable inventions;
    - compulsory licensing; and
    - government use provisions.

13 The Standard Patent – Application Procedures and Filing Requirements

Application procedures

Phase 1 – Application in the designated patent office:

- Application for grant of a patent in a designated patent office or an international application under the PCT designating a designated patent office; and
- Publication of the designated patent application by the designated patent office or publication or other notification by the designated patent office which serves to indicate the entry into the national phase of an international application under the PCT.

Phase 2 – Application in Hong Kong at the first stage:

- Application in Hong Kong within six months of publication by a designated patent office or publication or other notification by the designated patent office which serves to indicate the entry into the national phase of an international application;
- recording in the register and publication of the request to record by the Registrar on compliance with the formality requirements; and
- maintenance of application on the anniversary of the date of filing of the designated patent application falling in the fifth year after the publication of the request to record and thereafter annually provided the designated patent application is still pending in the designated patent office.

Phase 3 – Application procedures in the designated patent office:

- Substantive search and examination in designated patent office; and
- Grant of designated patent.

If the designated patent application is refused or deemed withdrawn the standard patent cannot be granted in Hong Kong and the standard patent application cannot be maintained.

Phase 4 – Application procedures in Hong Kong at the second stage:

- Application in Hong Kong within six months of grant of designated patent of a request to record the designated patent and grant of standard patent; and
- Recording in the register of the designated patent and grant of the standard patent and publication by the Registrar, on compliance with the formality requirements.

The flowchart below summarises the overall application procedures for obtaining a standard patent in Hong Kong.

OBTAINING A STANDARD PATENT IN HONG KONG

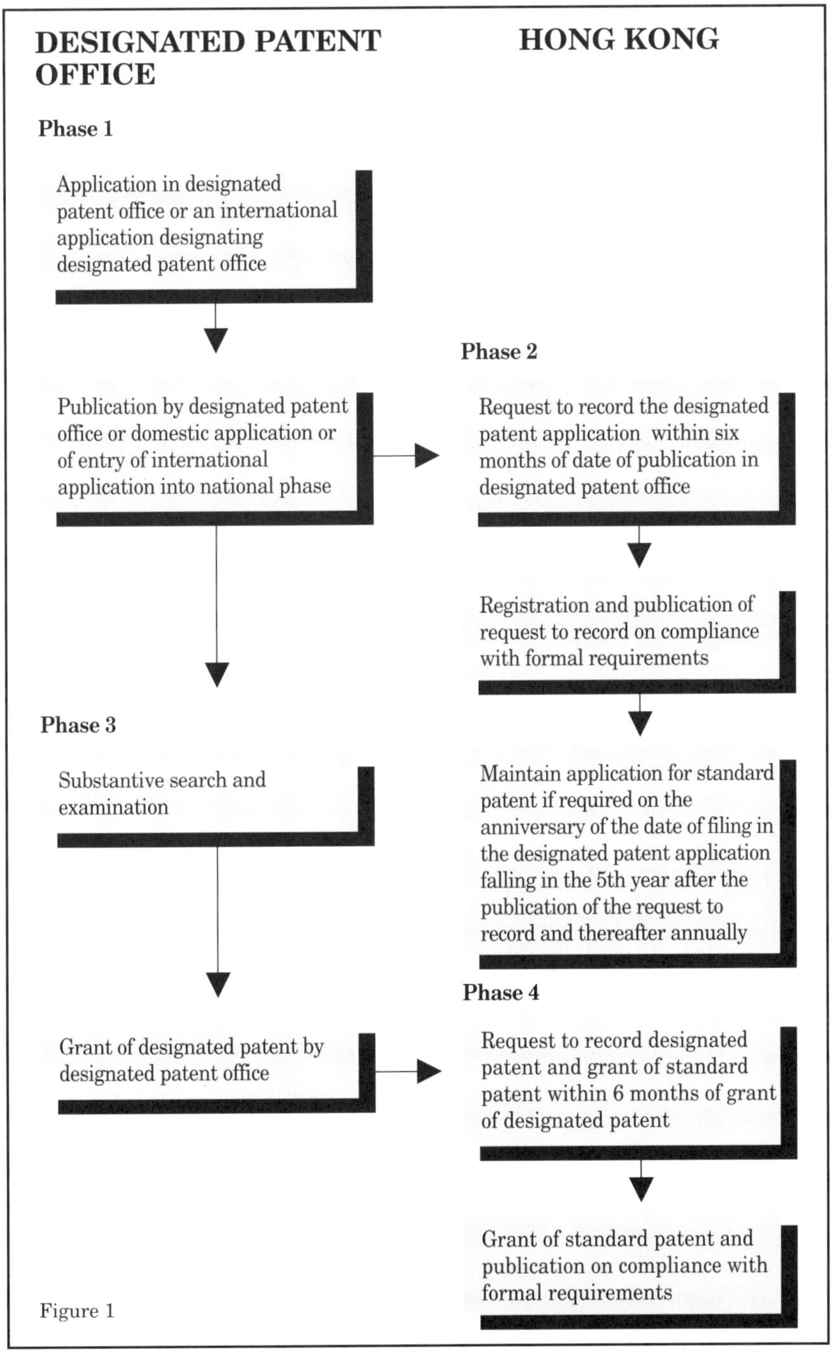

Figure 1

First Stage Filing Requirements in Hong Kong

At the first stage the following must be filed:

- An application form in either English or Chinese;
- Certain documents in support; and
- A filing fee and advertisement fee.

First Stage – Application Form Requirements

- The name and address of the applicant in English or Chinese with a transliteration into the roman alphabet of the Chinese name;
- If the applicant is not the current applicant named in the designated patent application a statement indicating his right to apply;
- The title of the invention in English and Chinese;
- Specified details of the designated patent application or the international application, ie
  - application and publication number of designated patent application or international application;
  - date of filing in designated patent office or of the international application; and
  - date of publication of designated patent application or the date of publication or other notification by the designated patent office which serves to indicate entry into the national phase of an international application;
- If the application is divided or derived from an earlier Hong Kong application certain specified details;
- If the benefit of the priority right accorded in the designated patent office is claimed under s 98 of the *Patents Ordinance* a statement of such claim and information as to
  - the country in which priority is claimed;
  - the application number of the prior application on which the application for priority is claimed;
  - the date of filing of such prior application; and
  - in the case of an international application whether the claim is based on a right of priority claimed in the designated patent office or claimed in the international application and accepted in the designated patent office;
- If the inventor is not named in the designated patent application, the name of the inventor with a transliteration if given in Chinese;

- If the benefit of a claim made in the designated patent application in respect of any non-prejudicial disclosure is to be claimed in Hong Kong, specified information;
- Name and address of the agent, if any;
- Address for service; and
- Request to enter a record of the designated patent application in the register.

The form must be signed by the applicant or his agent.

First Stage – Documents to be Filed in Support

- A photocopy, unverified, of the designated patent application as published by the designated patent office or the international application as published by World Intellectual Property Organisation;
- A duplicate copy of the designated patent application as published by the designated patent office or of the international application as published by the World Intellectual Property Organisation in loose-leaf form;
- Where the designated patent application is based on an international application further specified documents, ie
    - a verified copy of any translation of the international application published by the designated patent office; and
    - a verified copy of any publication of information in the designated patent office concerning the international application;
- If the applicant is not the current applicant named in the designated patent application, information indicating the derivation of the right of the applicant to apply in Hong Kong; and
- Translation of the Abstract as contained in the international application or in the designated patent application as published, if any, into the other official language or into both official languages if such abstract is not in the official language.

First Stage – Filing Fee and Advertisement Fee

The filing fee and the advertisement fees are set by the *Patents (General) Rules*.

Second Stage Filing Requirements in Hong Kong

At the second stage the following will be required:

- An application form in the language in which the request to record was made which will be the language of the proceedings;
- Certain documents in support; and
- A filing fee and advertisement fee.

Second Stage – Application Form Requirements

- Details of the corresponding request to record, ie
  - application number;
  - publication number;
  - date of publication; and
  - the name and address of the applicant;
- If the language of the proceedings is Chinese the name will also have to be given in the roman alphabet;
- If the applicant is not the current applicant recorded in the register or is not the proprietor named in the designated patent, a statement indicating the derivation of the right of the applicant to make the request for registration and grant;
- Title of the invention in English and Chinese;
- Specified details of the designated patent application, ie
  - the publication number allocated to the designated patent by the designated patent office; and
  - the date of grant of the designated patent.
- Name and address of the agent, if any;
- If the applicant does not have an address in Hong Kong, an address for service in Hong Kong; and
- Request to register the designated patent and grant a standard patent.

Second Stage - Documents in Support

- A verified copy of the designated patent as published;
- A duplicate copy of the designated patent application as published in loose-leaf form; and
- If the applicant is not the current applicant for the standard patent recorded in the register or is not the proprietor named in the designated patent, a statement indicating the derivation of the right of the applicant to apply in Hong Kong and prescribed documents in support.

Filing Fee and Advertisement Fee

The filing fee and the advertisement fee as set in the *Patents (General) Rules*.

14 The Short-term Patent – Application Procedures and Filing Requirements

Application procedures

Application may be made by any person or his agent to the Registrar by filing

- a request for a grant of a short-term patent ;
- an application form in English or Chinese;
- certain documents in support; and
- filing and advertisement fees.

The flowchart below summarises the overall application procedures for obtaining a standard patent in Hong Kong.

How to Obtain a Short-term Patent

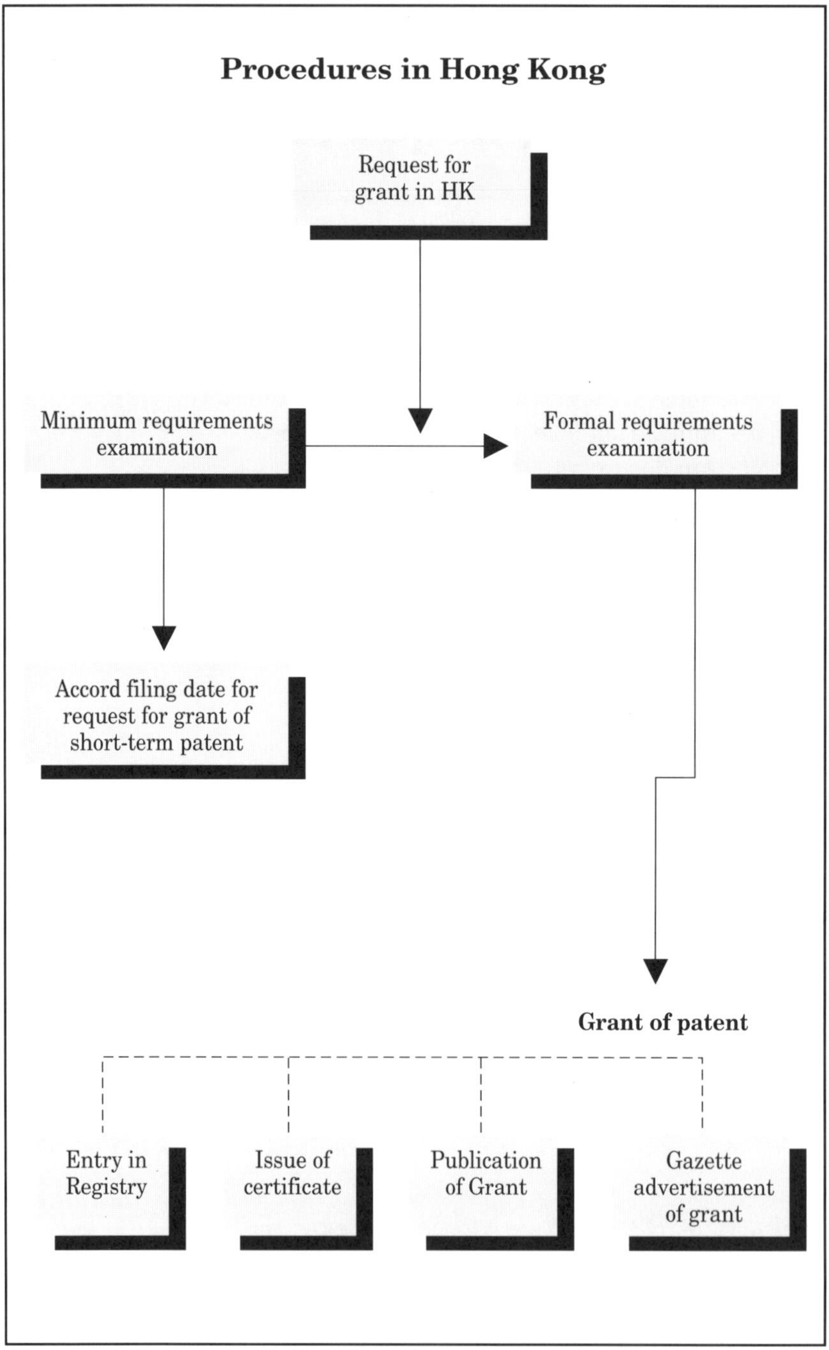

Application Form requirements

An application form specified by the Registrar under s 150 of the *Patents Ordinance* in the Notice of Specification of Forms must contain the following information:

- The reference of the applicant's agent;
- The name and address of the applicant which may be given in English or Chinese but if the name is given in Chinese characters a transliteration of the name must also be given in the roman alphabet;
- The title of the invention which should be short and indicate the matter to which the patent relates;
- The classification of the invention according to the International Patent Classification up to the subclass level and also indicating the edition number of the IPC used;
- If the invention requires the use of a micro-organism for its performance, details of the
  - (i) depository institution;
  - (ii) date of deposit with such institution; and
  - (iii) accession number of the deposit;
- If the application for a short-term patent is based on an international application the following information is required:
  - (i) international application number given by the International Bureau of the World Intellectual Property Organisation;
  - (ii) the international filing date accorded to the international application;
  - (iii) the publication number of the international application allocated by the International Bureau of the World Intellectual Property Organisation;
  - (iv) the date of entry into the national phase in the Chinese Patent Office of the international application;
  - (v) the date of issuance of the National Application Notification by the Chinese Patent Office (if applicable); and
  - (vi) the application number of the Chinese patent application (if known);
- If the application is divided or is derived from an earlier Hong Kong application, then the relevant section of the *Patents Ordinance* under which application is made must be stated together with the following information:

(i) the earlier application number in Hong Kong; and
(ii) the date of filing of the earlier application in Hong Kong;

- If the benefit of the right of priority accorded in the designated patent office is to be claimed under s 111 of the *Patents Ordinance*, then the form must state this and give
  (i) the country in which priority is claimed;
  (ii) the application number of the prior application on which the application for priority is claimed; and
  (iii) the date of filing of such prior application;
- The name and the last known address of the person the applicant believes to be the inventor. If the name of the inventor is only given in Chinese characters a transliteration of the name must also be given in the roman alphabet;
- If a claim under s 109 *Patents Ordinance* is made in the designated patent application in respect of any non-prejudicial disclosure and it is wished to claim the benefit in Hong Kong, then the form must state this and give the following information in respect of the claim:
  (i) the name and place of the exhibition;
  (ii) the opening date of such exhibition; and
  (iii) the date of the first disclosure of the invention;
- Indicate if a request for deferral is made and the period for which deferral is required. If this is not specifically stated it will be taken that a deferral is not requested;
- The form must state the documents in support and the number of sheets of these documents. This is an administrative requirement;
- The name and address of the applicant's agent, if any, and an address for service in Hong Kong if the applicant does not have an address in Hong Kong; and
- A request to grant a short-term patent.

The form must be completed in either English or Chinese. The language which is used on the form will be the language of the proceedings. The form must be signed by the applicant or his agent.

Documents in support

The following documents will be required to be filed in support of the application.

- The specification which shall contain
  - (i) the description;
  - (ii) the claim or claims; and
  - (iii) the drawings (if any);
- An abstract of the invention in both English and Chinese which contains a concise summary of the matter contained in the specification and any relevant drawings;
- A verified copy of the previous application on which the claim to priority is based and a translation into the language of the proceedings of such priority documents if it is not in one of the official languages;
- The search report and if it is not in an official language a translation into the language of the proceedings;
- In the case of an application based on an international application instead of the documents outlined in para 1 above, the following documents are required:
  - (i) a photocopy of the international application as published by the International Bureau of the World Intellectual Property Organisation;
  - (ii) photocopy of the international search report;
  - (iii) photocopy of the translation of the international application if any published by the Chinese Patent Office;
  - (iv) photocopy of any information with regard to the international application published by the Chinese Patent Office; and
  - (v) a copy of the National Application Notification issued by the Chinese Patent Office; and
- A statement of inventorship on the form set in the Rules showing how the applicant derived the right to the patent from the inventor.

Filing Fee and advertisement fee

The filing fee and the advertisement fee as set in Schedule 1 to the *Patents (General) Rules*.

Index